FIVE GUYS Named ZAIKA

SHUIAB KHAN

First published in Great Britain in 2021
Copyright © Shuiab Khan

The moral right of this author has been asserted.
All rights reserved.

No part of this publication may be reproduced, stored in a retrieval system, or transmitted, in any form or by any means, without the prior permission in writing of the publisher, nor be otherwise circulated in any form of binding or cover other than that in which it is published and without a similar condition including this condition being imposed on the subsequent purchaser.

Typesetting and publishing by
UK Book Publishing
www.ukbookpublishing.com
ISBN: 978-1-914195-21-1

In memory of

Umbreen Ali
1975-2020
Journalist, writer and columnist

Contents

1 Paul

2 Christmas Eve 1997

3 Pub Quiz

4 Paperboy

5 The set up

6 A game you must play

7 Custard Creams

8 Our town

9 This is Dickens Street not Fleet Street

10 Rustam

11 Zaika S. Akkas

12 Contrary to popular opinion

13 Book Girl

14 Freshie

15 Journalism for dummies

16 Mind your language

17 Do we not deserve Coke?

18 Cheque Please

19 It's a scam isn't it?

20 Indian-Pakistani

21 Take it or leave it

22 T-Bone

23 Carry on Cleo

24 Football

25 Jaffa Cakes

26 The suit

27 Women's stuff

28 Doesn't it

29 A friend in need

30 Chapati

31 The usual suspects

32 The Last Bit

33 Book girl again

34 One rule for one

35 The Yukka plant

36 Worf is not a sell out

37 Deadline

38 One Night in Blackburn

Some names and identifying details have been changed to protect the privacy of individuals. I may have changed identifying characteristics and details such as physical properties, occupations and places of residence. I have tried to recreate events and conversations from my memories of them. Some dialogues have been re-imagined and some incidents may have taken place outside the time frame within this story.

Foreword

Many in Lancashire and Greater Manchester will remember The Asian Image as an informative and witty local newspaper. It became all of those things and more. This is the story of its conception and birth–told naturally and unapologetically.

The events chronicled are funny, audacious and shine a light on life in late 1990s Lancashire which unless you lived through that period you wouldn't recognise.

The is a story of five friends, talented but at risk of losing hope and direction as they soon realise they may have bitten off more than they can chew. It is a story of their audacious belief that they could start and master a project of mammoth proportions – to print a newspaper and distribute it themselves door-to-door to thousands of households – in 30 days.

Their journey during that first month is revealing of closed social attitudes but also details how intrepid determination, persistence and 'winging it', can and did win the day.

The Asian Image challenged social ideas, self-styled community representatives and religious norms. But equally it celebrated the community's many achievements with aplomb and unmitigated joy.

It is no exaggeration to say that the newspaper, which still publishes online today, became part of the cultural narrative of Lancashire and Greater Manchester. Its ability to stay independent can be traced back to its beginnings and the young men behind its creation. This is their story of unrivalled triumph through tribulation.

Mo the Barrister – (I'm in Chapter 31)

1 PAUL

We like to measure being offended on different levels because the truth is some things are more offensive than others. With deadline day looming it was time to speak to as many businesses as possible and to get out of our comfort zones.

Anyone involved in sales will tell you it is not easy trying to sell something to someone who has no idea who you are and what you are trying to offload. It is a thankless task but when your wage and whole existence depends on making the sale the pressure can be suffocating. Nobody wants to go back to the office having failed.

It was a typically cold and windy January day as I stood inside a phone box patiently waiting for someone to answer a call. "Come on, pick up. Hi, Hello." On this particular morning, I had made an appointment at a furniture company to see if I could coax the business into advertising in the first edition of our newspaper. "I have a meeting at 11.30 and was just checking to see if that was all in order." The woman confirmed the time was correct, listing my name and company. "Yes, that's correct. Thank You… thank you."

As someone who was always late for appointments, unusually I had made an effort to arrive here at least ten minutes early and was asked to wait in reception. I sat myself down with a black folder on my lap.

I peered down at my new shoes again. They were good-looking shoes. It is difficult finding a good pair of shoes that look presentable but are also functional. When you are 24 and have achieved nothing of note, things like this matter and first impressions can make all the difference, I had thought. Maybe the goatee beard was a little too informal?

Twenty minutes passed, which did not seem to be too bad considering once I had sat around for an hour only to be told the person I had come to meet had gone to lunch. At the time I had wanted to get upset but then ended up apologising myself and making another appointment with the same person. That's what happens when you are desperate to make a sale.

I began to think back to the summer just gone. I had just returned from Ecuador where I had spent a few months teaching English to a class full of women. It was a pretty easy job and at first, I had not really taken it seriously and treated it like a bit of fun. I had no class plan and spent the first two days teaching them slang words. English, even if it came from my mouth, was a highly sought-after commodity and it felt good to be the centre of attention for a change. Things changed on the Friday after the first week had ended when the class lined up to pay their fees. They worked during the day and saved their money to attend an evening class three times a week so they could learn a new language and there I was treating the whole thing like a joke. I did not repeat the mistakes of the first week again.

Eventually, the receptionist came over and asked me to follow her into a large boardroom area.

Two men walked in and stared at me. "Paul is it?"

I stood up. "Yes, that's right."

Both sat opposite me and looked over at me again. The blond man with a stubble looked at the scruffy pad he was holding. "Paul?"

I had not been able to get an appointment and had decided to rename myself Paul. 'Shuiab' was difficult to pronounce and it had failed to get me a meeting on two occasions. It was not easy getting yourself at a table to speak to potential advertisers.

So, 'Paul' was born.

It was far less insulting than what my friend Khalil had attempted already. When making some calls he had pretended to be 'camp' in the hope it would help him close the sale. I must admit it worked a charm for him and he felt people were less likely to be threatened by him. Yes, I understand how offensive that might sound.

"Yes, Paul.' I smiled. "But you can call me Paulee if you want. That's my nickname."

Paulee? That must be the nerves.

"Okay then." The plump man looked across at his colleague. "So, this paper, is it an Asian paper for Asians only?"

Great, some interest in the product already. "We are targeting Asian readers and anyone who wants to read it really."

I handed them the sheet of A4 paper listing the prices. I am certain anyone else trying to sell advertising space in a newspaper would be armed with a whole set of figures and graphics with which to wow the potential customer. I had none. We had not printed a single issue and all I had was this one piece of paper. Deep down I knew this was not enough and wished I had made more of an effort in both what I brought to the party and the way I had dressed.

The blond man peered down at the sheet. "Is it in English?"

"Yes, all in English and with local news and sport."

They looked at the sheet again. There wasn't much information on there if I was going to be honest; I wasn't entirely sure why it required more than one look.

The blond man sighed to himself. "The thing is, and I don't know how to put this, but we don't really want Asian customers."

It was the kind of comment I had heard on the phone but to hear it from someone sat in front of you was different.

Being offended, as I said, was measured in levels. There were those who were racist towards you to your face and there were those who would rather do it behind your back. And there were those who didn't actually think there was anything wrong with what they were saying because they themselves don't see it as being offensive.

At school I had been best friends with Chang. We had gone through primary school together and then on to secondary school and were inseparable. There were incidents of racism growing up for many of us, but I always imagined it was far worse for him as he I felt he went through more than I ever did. The thing was, he was at the wrong end of subtle racism by whites as well as other Asians due to his Chinese background. So, when I ended up measuring abuse, I would always do it by those standards. I guess it was my way of not having to contend with aggressive situations or challenge people.

We only had one apparent 'abuser' and here was a person who managed to take grief from all sides in his stride. He never let it show and always had a real sense of respect for himself whatever the circumstance.

One time, we were both on a bus on the way to see another friend of ours and sat on the top deck of the bus. Two white boys walked past and one of them smacked me on the side of the face and told us both to get off the bus. Chang knew all too well we would not win this fight and immediately intervened and asked them to leave the bus quickly as it didn't stop for long and they would miss their stop. It worked. It was almost as if he had been trained from a young age to deal with horrible incidents of this nature. Afterwards he even wanted to apologise on behalf of the two older boys because it was him who had wanted us to get on this bus.

In the office, I stared back at the two men sat in front of me. "You don't want any Asians in here. Can I ask why?"

The older man spoke up. "They don't spend anything. They come in here and browse and waste our time."

"I see. Things are changing, you have some great products in here and there are a lot of Asian families now who have a lot of disposable income. Well, maybe you have got it wrong," I said, hoping it would re-evaluate their attitudes towards 'Asians'.

The second man was not convinced. "Maybe we haven't and maybe we know our business better than you do."

He was right, I didn't know their business.

This was going from bad to worse but even I wasn't going to try to rescue this sale. "So let's get this straight: it is not as if you don't like Asians, but you just think they are not good spenders. I'm sure you have nothing against people from an Asian background; they just waste your time."

"Yeah, you got it," The larger of the two men said smiling, relieved that I had cracked the code. "We have nothing against your sort at all but the last time we had a few in here they did smell of curry."

I tried my best to hide my disdain. "So, you think that Asian folk are tight-fisted and come in here stinking up the place. You definitely don't need to be advertising in an Asian paper for Asians then, do you."

Both men seemed a little taken aback by my comment.

"I think you have worked it out. No offence, though you seem to be different."

Clearly my attempt at sarcasm had gone right over their heads.

"What do you mean different? What makes me different?"

Why I decided to take on the role of the character Tommy DeVito played by Joe Pesci in the film, *Goodfellas* I have no idea. It was probably a way of masking my real feelings.

The two looked at each other before the blond one said, "You know… you are err, different?"

"How so? What makes me so special."

The second man intervened. "Well, you seem to be named Paul for instance. That's different."

I scratched the side of my head. "Yes, yes, it is. It is a great name, isn't it."

There was an awkward silence. It is easy when people say they would have made some witty comment and walked away having put these two people in their place. Reality isn't like that at all.

In reality, we don't say the things we should. In reality, we walk away with the tail between our legs.

"Okay then," I said. "It was good of you to see me but if you do change your mind in the future then call the number at the bottom of the sheet."

"That's wonderful." And both men started talking to one another behind me as I got up and left the room.

Paul never made an appearance again.

2 CHRISTMAS EVE 1997

Anything of any note and importance normally begins with a conversation about something else.

In our case we were talking about people and why some of them had this need to draw attention to themselves for having achieved very little in life.

"I met one of the Haseeb brothers the other day. He says he is setting up a new technology firm and is expanding into several towns." Khalil – or Kal for short – a year younger than me and my best friend, had always had an entrepreneurial side to him from a very young age and loved to predict the future of technology.

"He is on to something, you know. You see this phone here, this is the big thing at the moment."

I wasn't convinced. "It is will never catch on. A mobile phone? I don't have no mobile and do I look like a guy who can't get by?"

"You really want me to answer that?" Kal smirked.

He was right. I was not getting by but this mobile phone lark was just something for the yuppies. I still used the word 'yuppies' to describe people who were only interested in making money and then wanted to flaunt that wealth in my face.

"Yeah, but this whole phone thing. Why would I need to be in touch with someone all the time? If anyone wants to speak to me, they can knock at my house or call me at home."

Knocking on someone's door at each other's houses was something we had both done since we were kids and that was never going to change. In my case it was fraught with real difficulty as I would always attempt to hide the fact that my friends were at the door. My mother had this idea we would be up to no good; in reality, we were doing something far more mundane – playing football in the surrounding alleyways.

It wasn't the same when I would go and knock at Kal's house. He was almost relieved that someone had made the effort to come to his home to get him out. It wasn't as if he hated being home, but I was kind of a get out clause for him at times.

"I am going out to play with Shuiab."

It was the perfect exit. No worries.

It was a surprise that Kal had even managed to get through and live to his twenties. A reckless personality, he had spent his school years and much of his time at college trying to stay out of trouble. How he had got through those teenage years without having caused serious harm to himself and those around him remained a mystery. It was only when he was forced to work long hours in his family's factory whilst his friends left the town did the penny finally drop.

"The fact is, we want to be seen as social animals, but in reality we want to be left alone." I was trying to defend my earlier statement in the hope it would make me seem less of a young man who was being left behind with the times.

"Also, people like Haseeb always brag about their mediocre achievements when you meet them. They want you to talk about their life and how important it is in the hope it will impress you. I can tell you now I am not impressed."

A blue Vauxhall Astra pulled up outside and we could see Zak and Akeel getting out of the vehicle. We had agreed to meet at a takeaway to have some chicken and chips – something that made us feel we had had a night out.

Blackburn was experiencing a mini boom in halal food joints and this particular one had become one of our favourite haunts.

Zak was always impeccably dressed whilst Akeel (sometimes renamed 'Aki' for short) tended to be the complete opposite. He was one of those people who would turn up to someone's wedding wearing the same ripped jeans and tight-fitting Asian style kameez (shirt). He did this on purpose because he honestly was not bothered who looked at him and he cared little for people's perceptions of him. It was a quality that I never found in anyone else I had ever met. Today he had on his trademark Yasser Arafat scarf and denim jacket despite the bitterly cold wind.

Zak, meanwhile, always made an effort. Even a short trip to the takeaway mattered. It wasn't as if he was into labels but everything was downplayed as if to say 'I want you to notice me for the way I am rather than the label I have'. How these two people found themselves in each other's company was a mystery to me at times. Yet, it worked.

They both made their way in and sat down taking the seats on either side of us at the table.

Zak introducing himself with his customary, 'Ow'do'

"What's it going to be today, gentlemen?" I asked.

Akeel sighed. "Let me see, this is a chicken place that serves halal chicken so make mine a halal chicken."

Kal meanwhile was scanning through the menu.

Zak looked at him. "Anything new?"

"I am thinking."

Having made the decision to come out, I always counted down the minutes when I could return home. "What is there to think about? We have been here fifty times and we always order the same meal. There is chicken and there is chicken and chips. And there is, lo and behold, more chicken."

Akeel joined in. "Yeah, just order the bloody burger and be done with it."

'Bloody', I felt, was a very northern term, despite it having a wider use. You could travel the world and you would never see anyone else using the word 'bloody' in almost every sentence as much as us. Bloody was our word and I felt sometimes it helped to set us apart from the rest of the more dignified people on the planet.

Kal continued to look at the menu as if to suggest that he didn't want to be rushed into a decision he might later regret.

"Come on, Kal, we haven't got all day."

"Why? Have you got anywhere to go?"

I had nowhere to go. I was not busy. I did not need to be home. It was only 8 o'clock and in a town like Blackburn there is very little to do on a Wednesday night. In all honestly there is nothing to do on any night of the week in this town.

It was Christmas Eve and we were looking forward to watching some television and lounging around in our front rooms.

"Have you pencilled in what you are going to watch in the Radio Times?"

Zak loved to talk about the little nostalgic things that many of us took for granted. It probably helped to remind him of a time when things weren't so bad. The pencilling in of a listing in the Radio Times and TV Times was something we had done since childhood. Although many of us had grown out of this habit, Zak, it seems, wanted us to believe that he still took part in this festive ritual.

"You still don't do that, do you?" asked Akeel.

"Of course I do. You can't have Christmas without marking out programmes in the Radio Times."

I had to interject. "Even I don't do that anymore, Zak. It's so eighties."

"It isn't. The Two Ronnies Christmas Show is on tomorrow."

"Yeah, my point. They always have the Two Ronnies Christmas special on or some repeat. Is there a time they didn't have the Two Ronnies on at Christmas? Or Only Fools and Horses? It is the same shit every year."

"I like the Two Ronnies. Proper funny penchods they are," added Akeel.

Swearing in Punjabi was an art. This particular word 'penchod' was regularly used in conjunction with other English words. We grew up in multi-lingual households and would fluently speak both languages but swear words had a place of their own in our culture. We would never use such words at home, of course, but amongst friends these disgusting terms (because that is what they were) were commonplace. There was of course a golden rule – one was never to swear in such a way at someone or a friend. The use of this particular filthy word had once led to a small riot between cricketers at the local park when the bowler had accidentally uttered it to a batter. Let's just say this was very ill-advised as it was the batter who had the 'offensive weapon' in his hand at the time.

I learnt most of my slurs and swears at a young age whilst on a trip to Pakistan when I came across a great uncle of mine who could find the right swear word for almost any situation. Once I witnessed him swear at a man on a donkey and he even had a put down for the poor animal.

Punjabi by its very nature is a brutal language and in our world it separated the classes. We conversed in Punjabi as we felt it was the language of the masses whilst the more eloquent Urdu was spoken by 'high society' types, or so I thought. I don't know if there was any truth in this, but it helped us feel slightly more in tune with the common man. Anyway, has anyone ever really seen or heard someone swear in Urdu? I certainly hadn't.

Kal mulled over the menu. "I think I will have the half chicken and chips."

"Are you sure?" quipped Zak.

"Errm, I don't know. Yes, I will go for the chicken and chips."

I hurried over to the counter and placed the orders. "Can we have three chicken and chips and one burger and chips."

I sat back down and there was for once an embarrassing silence. Kal and I had spent years perfecting these silences but it didn't seem right when there were others around us. I could go an hour in the company of Kal and not speak to him and we were comfortable with it. Why people need to talk when there is nothing to say was beyond me. We should be able to sit in silence and be done with it.

Zak didn't like the silences. "Not been that bad this winter, has it?"

It certainly says a lot about any situation when you end up talking about the weather. Most places I had travelled to were unlikely to ever use another familiar term, 'It's nice out'.

I had to say something of note. "Is this it?"

"Is what it?" said Kal.

"This what we are doing here. This, sat around in this shitty takeaway talking about the weather?"

No one was surprised by this question of mine. I had a habit of bringing the conversation down a more basic level. "It is Christmas Eve and here we are sat here doing nothing."

"What do you want to do, dress up like Santa and hand out presents?" Akeel asked.

"Why did I come back to this town? There is nothing for us here. Anyone who has any sense should get up and leave whenever they get the opportunity."

"Yeah, it is shit really." Kal was as honest as they came. He took off his black leather jacket and placed it on the seat behind him and then decided it was too cold in the takeaway and promptly put it back on again.

The problem with Blackburn is that it didn't really have anything going for it. Apart from the football team which had 'put it on the map' there was little else for anyone growing up here. In the middle of winter it was at best a desolate place to be and with Ramadan on the horizon things were going to get even more desperate. The town had come through a tough decade and the nineties had begun positively with the football team defying all logic and winning the premiership. But it was with note that we read negative reviews of this famous victory in the press. They didn't want us to win really. They hated that this shithole of a town had taken their precious trophy away from the more fashionable teams.

Behind the glory of the football, we were all suffering. There really was nothing to do and the future looked bleak.

"Do you know what, Kal? We should leave."

Kal looked up at me.

Akeel always managed to put a smile on our faces by saying something so profound. "You know what they say, wherever you go, you will take your own sorry arse with you."

I spotted Qadir walking towards the takeaway. "Oh no, everyone prepare to slap some hands."

Qadir was a likeable chap but he had strange habits.

"Oh dear," said Kal and took his phone out of his pocket.

"Why, what's the matter?" said a confused looking Akeel.

Qadir headed to the counter to pick up his food, paid and then spotted us in the corner.

The thing with Qadir was, he liked to hold out his hand every time he agreed with something. If one did not then 'slap' his hand he would move on to the next person until someone touched his palm with their own palm. It was a sight to behold and for a newbie it could be quite disorientating.

Qadir walked over to us.

"Hey, Qadir, how's it going today?" I could see Kal still fiddling with his phone.

"All is good, all is good. What you boys doing? I see."

I was waiting for a mundane anecdote and the customary 'holding out of the hand' but it was not forthcoming.

"Okay then I see you guys later, I have to go," and he headed for the exit.

"Wow, what was all that about?" And then I noticed Kal was still fiddling with his phone. "Anything you want to tell us, Kal?"

Kal put his phone on the table and then chuckled to himself, which normally meant he was hiding something. "Okay here it is. I may have upset him last week. He kept holding out his hand like this every time there was a punchline." Kal held out his hand in front of Akeel who seemed even more confused. "And I just got annoyed and told him to stop doing it."

"You didn't?' said Zak.

I was shocked but not surprised. "Why would you do that? That's his thing. Everyone has a thing. You can't take people's things away from them. He tells the anecdote, holds out his hand and you slap it.

How hard can that be?"

Kal shook his head and frowned. "I just couldn't take it anymore. In a two-minute conversation he held out his hand eight times. Eight times is far too many."

Most people refrain from saying what is on their mind because they do not wish to offend the other person. But not Kal. He couldn't stop himself from being totally honest, which led to some people not taking a liking to him and others respecting him even more. I, on the other hand, would put up with the annoyance even if it would cause me unnecessary pain and anguish.

"Anyway, why are you so hung up about Fiesta?" said Kal.

A nickname was something we were all used to. Thankfully, I had managed to escape being branded in such a way. Others sadly had not. My favourite nickname had to be 'Keegan' – a man named after Kevin Keegan not for his footballing prowess but more for the fact he had hair like Kevin Keegan when he was younger. It was the only nickname I wish I had been stuck with myself. I mean, who doesn't want to be named after am England legend?

Akeel frowned. "Fiesta? I thought his name was Qadir?"

"Yeah yeah. He got caught using his dad's Fiesta when he was a kid so we called him Fiesta," said Kal.

Zak laughed as if to suggest he had heard of the incident then went silent realising he may not have actually come across this momentous moment in time.

"So what?" asked Akeel.

Kal: "What do you mean so what?"

"Yeah, so what? Did he crash it or something?"

"Crash what?" said a confused Kal.

"The Fiesta?"

Kal smiled. "It wasn't that type of Fiesta."

Zak laughed out loud again and I stared across at Kal.

"Forget it, Aki," I interrupted. "Brother needs help."

Kal sniggered again. Then stopped and smiled again for good measure.

"You know I was thinking of joining the Royal Air Force." This took everyone by surprise. I had earlier in the week visited the local recruiting centre. If nothing else I thought it would help me see the world and get me out of the town.

Zak seemed alarmed at the revelation. "You what?"

"Yeah I went to have a look. I had an appointment and everything. Really nice guy."

Kal was never one to discount any of my grand claims. "Captain Shuiab Khan. Sounds good."

"No, Group Captain Shuiab Khan," I replied.

"You don't want to do that." Thankfully Zak said something I was thinking.

"No, it looks good. I am little afraid of heights, but I think if you put your mind to something you can do anything."

"You should keep applying."

"There is nothing out there, Zak. Look, we did everything by the book and where did it get us?"

"Relax, something will come up." Akeel attempted to cheer me up.

"Yeah, there's bound to be something you are good at."

"You know, I just realised something I am actually quite good at: nothing. I am the nothing guy. I have a certain set of skills but these are of no use to anyone. I don't even have enough money to pay for this meal."

Akeel leaned forward. "No one has enough money to pay for this meal."

I was having none of it. "The point is it is time to get real. We have messed about enough."

Kal tried his next tactic. "You make your own luck."

"You sound like a knobhead."

"Fuck you then."

Conversations had a habit of descending into anarchy. It was probably why we managed to get by for so long and remain such good friends. We could essentially say what we wanted and how we wanted to each other, but nothing ever came between us.

Zak as always decided to break up the mini fight. "Just cut it out."

But I wasn't having anything of it. "You know that interview I went to for British Airways last week. I know for sure the bird got the job. Even I would not hire me. I would hire her. If I was the manager, I would hire her and just come in every day and stand in the car park to watch her go to work."

"You know, that sounds exactly like something you would do," chuckled Kal. Then frowned. "It also sounds proper screwed in the head."

Zak who always liked to raise the level of conversation before things went south. "You can't refer to women as birds."

I glanced across at him and smirked knowing full well I had only said it to annoy him.

The takeaway owner walked across and began to place the meals on the table.

"Salaam, uncle, how are things?" Akeel asked.

He had overheard us and had an idea for us. "Why don't you guys set up a newsletter?"

Kal looked up at him. "What?"

"Yeah a newsletter. A Pakistani newsletter for Pakistanis. You are intelligent fellows who knows English."

Some still felt that speaking English was a bonus and meant you were more likely to be a success. How little did they know.

Kal glanced across at Zak. "That's not a bad idea actually. A newsletter? A newspaper would be better. Zak, you know about newspapers. You used to do one?"

Zak had published a newspaper and named it the Lancashire Independent. "Yeah, but that was a different time. Too many big heads wanted to be 'Big Ed'. It was a student one at most and it is not easy. The hardest thing is funding it. You need to get ads."

Akeel looked interested. "We can get adverts. We just sell it, don't we?"

Zak was still a little hesitant. "It is not exactly that easy. But I guess it could work."

Kal swapped his chicken and chips with Akeel's burger and chips. He then drowned his chips in garlic and ketchup.

I stared at him. "Why must you do that?"

"What?"

"That. There," pointing at his chips and burger. "Why must you your ruin your meal. Just put the sauce at the side and dip it in."

You could tell a lot about a person from how he ate. Kal ate all his food in a random order whilst I liked to have a system in place. He shook his head and then proceeded to open his burger bun and place chips on top of the burger and squirting more sauce on top, glancing up at me as he did it.

Akeel laughed at us both.

Kal was warming to the newspaper idea. "We sell the adverts and then you can write it and print it. Selling isn't that hard as long as you have a focus."

Zak began to cut open his chicken pieces one at a time. "It can be done. But you have to keep it going. That is the hardest part. You can't just print one. May I remind you there is no money in it at the beginning."

Akeel was already excited. "Fuck it, let's do it."

Akeel was an enigma wrapped within a mystery. He never left the town and spent most of the nineties just trying to get by. It never really bothered him he should try to get some qualifications and it kind of didn't matter so much. If he had put his mind to it, he would have comfortably outdone all of his peers.

"That's the attitude. You up for it?" Kal looked at me.

I was not too sure. I was never any good at English. "Number one I got a 'D' in English – twice – and number two we can't do just a Pakistani newspaper – what about all the Indians? Anyway, Zak is the only one here who knows anything about newspapers."

I felt Zak had maybe secretly harboured that one day he would be able to publish another newspaper, "What is there to know? We write the stuff and print it."

"That might be the case," I said. "Yeah. We don't know anything about how a newspaper is printed."

"Is it still that machine?" said a hesitant Kal. "Honestly, I don't know? That machine that presses the letters and you turn the handle."

"Like in cowboy films?" He surely didn't think that newspapers were still printed on those machines.

In fact, Kal did. "Yes, you know what I'm on about, Zak? They press the letters in one by one."

"Are you serious?" said a concerned Zak. "It's 1997 not 1887. You design it on a computer programme, print it and lay them on grid sheets. Then take it to the printers who will put them on plates. We just need a computer and a camera."

"That's it?" Kal said in between mouthfuls. "Eat up then, lads, we have a newspaper to publish."

3 PUB QUIZ

"Okay, listen up, we need this one." Zak clicked his pen several times in anticipation.

Ever since a young age, Zak had been interested in two things: Liverpool Football Club and Stock Aitken and Waterman tracks. He had grown up in Blackburn and then gone on to gain an English and media degree before returning to the town. Anyone meeting him for the first time would not know he was Pakistani at all because he had an eczema skin condition which he had managed since a young age.

Every Monday we would head to the pub to take part in the quiz. It was not a familiar pub that you might find in inner city neighbourhoods, but situated just outside the town and it was probably the reason we were drawn to it.

The point is Muslims rarely ventured into pubs for obvious reasons, but this particular place, 'The Spread Eagle', hosted a quiz every so often and Zak being the ever resourceful one had persuaded us to take part. At first it seemed to be the nerdy thing to do and there was a danger also of being labelled 'gorafied', a term used to describe Zak on many an occasion. It meant that he was 'whitified' or had westernised habits. The funny thing was he tended to embrace the term because he was far from that in many ways and was probably more of a traditionalist than all of us put together. The truth was every second person who could string a few sentences together in their native tongue thought themselves more cultured than the next man. We also had the types who thought being a tad more religious than the next person gave them a reason to label everyone else 'a bit of a kafir'. Then we had those who would find any excuse to justify something because it made them feel less guilty about stuff. It was all bullshit, but no-one wanted to admit this to themselves.

The Spread Eagle wasn't the Queen Vic and the Rovers Return, but more of a smart, well-kept pub and restaurant frequented by what many would say were the more middle class, suburban types. Here, despite being the only Asians in the pub you didn't feel out of place. I guess it might come across as a bit snobbish but there was a safety in going somewhere a little more upmarket.

Every so often when a taxi-driver entered to pick up a fare we would turn our heads away in case he recognised us. Not that it really mattered if we got seen, but it was a natural reaction after having been told from an early age that you just don't venture into a place where 'beer is served'.

The quiz did give us an excuse to get out. Zak ordered the same drinks every single time – a couple of teas, a cola and an orange juice. We would find ourselves the same seats in the corner and after a while it was just like any other place where we could go and sit, chat and pretend to have been somewhere.

The quiz itself was hosted by Gerald, who would play a series of tracks and teams would have to guess the music from the several seconds that were playing. He was impeccable as always during the presentation and surprised me with his music choice.

Zak loved eighties music, whilst I always had a fascination from a young age for rock, pop and soul from the sixties and seventies. I had discovered my brother's vinyl record player and his very varied record collection and there was no looking back.

On this night, we had not been doing too well. Gerald played Oh Lori by the Alessi brothers – "Okay I can give you a little clue – spring, summer and fall."

Kal looked at me and shrugged his shoulders. "No way I know that."

Zak pretended as if to know the title and then also glanced at Akeel who said, "What? Why are you looking at me?"

Imran also turned to look at the others with a blank look on his face. "That's no qawwali that I know of."

Everyone knows pointless trivia they are not proud of. "That's 'Oh Lori' by…" I paused, "I don't know who it's by… some woman."

Zak nodded. "That's okay, we get one point. You sure?"

"Oh yes, definitely Oh Lori."

Gerald wound up the quiz for the night, "That's it for tonight. We are going to have a short break and then hand over your sheets to the table next to you."

Kal got up. "I need to take a piss and get the rounds in."

"Just don't do them in that order," said Zak.

"Yeah." I picked up my cup of tea. "I will have, let me see, another round of tea and my good friend Akeel will have an orange juice and maybe a tea for brother Imran here. And whilst you are up there, bring me some of those peanuts."

Kal shook his head.

Another reason the pub had been out of bounds was due to the unfounded belief that every single person in there must be either drunk or violent – or both. As we grew older, we had realised much of what we had been fed was in fact based on exaggeration and outright lies. Nonetheless it was frowned upon even if you popped in for a glass of cola.

Whenever we were in the Spread Eagle, Zak liked to recollect the story of the young men who had come home drunk one night. Imran and Akeel had not heard this particular tale. "Do you remember when we were kids there these two guys came smelling of booze and told their mums they had been stopped in the street and forced to drink alcohol?"

Imran and Akeel looked a little confused. "What the hell?" said Imran.

Imran, Akeel's older brother, had come to the country in the eighties and worked his way through school, college and university. Now 28, and several years older than the rest of us, he found himself helping on the launch of a newspaper.

"Yeah, their mums then went around the neighbourhood warning all the families we should all look out for some goray (white men) who were grabbing people at random and forcing them to drink alcohol. It scared the bloody pants off us. I wasn't allowed out for days," explained Zak.

Imran laughed. "You can't beat mums and their excuses. Always protecting the sons, no matter what."

Akeel still looked baffled. "So, did they catch them?"

"Who?" I said.

"The goray?"

Zak looked at him and frowned.

Akeel started laughing. "Oh I get it. Brilliant."

Kal returned from the bar with the orange juice and colas. "She's bringing the teas over in a bit."

Zak and Kal had earlier been discussing the launch of the newspaper. "So, we doing this then? The newspaper?" Kal was already planning a launch date.

"I suppose so." I still wasn't convinced it was something we could manage. "You guys were serious? I just thought that was just all male bravado. You know when that time we wanted to launch that halal pasty place?"

I had pointed out there were few halal eateries in the town centre and many Muslims could only opt for the cheese and onion options every time they went into Greggs the bakers. So, we had thought up an idea to open a halal pasty place. Kal had even come up with a really good name, 'Pasty Junction'.

"Hey, that is still a really good idea. But this we can do."

"Okay how's this going to pan out?" I said as the tea was placed on the table.

Zak had published a newspaper more as a hobby than anything

else. "The most important thing about printing a newspaper is not what goes into it but what adverts you have in it."

"I thought it was the headlines?" asked Akeel.

"Or the pictures," said Imran.

"We having a page 3?" I said.

"Oh yeah, an Asian paper with a page 3. What are going to have? Massi (pronounced Massee) in a bikini?" Zak joked

Everyone laughed.

"It could work." I added, "I would buy it. And for the ladies a shalwar kameez wearing man of the week complete with sandals and white socks."

"What's holding up the shalwar, nara or elastic?" said Zak. A nara was the rope that was inserted into the Asian style pants and then tied at the front. It was likely to be the most important piece of clothing ever thought up, but few spared a thought for this masterful invention. In recent years the 'nara' had been replaced by an elastic band that did not require tying and men who did opt for this 'false nara' were ridiculed by their contemporaries.

"What?" I asked.

"Is it an actual nara or an elastic?" reiterated Zak.

Imran smiled. "It is a genuine question: is the model on page 3 wearing an elastic or a nara in his pants?"

"It doesn't matter, does it?" I sighed. "Okay it is a nara because naras are far sexier."

Zak chuckled to himself. "Nice."

Sitting here amongst the 'locals', whilst Zak's stories always made for essential listening, Imran's Punjabi jokes really were something else and I could sense he was itching to tell one. There was nothing like it in the world. The Punjabi language in all its glory and the punchline would always sound more offensive every time it was retold.

"Tell us the one about the guy who wanted the lights switched off, Imy." I waited in anticipation. "I don't think Kal has heard it."

Imran leaned forward as if to limber up but didn't get the chance as the microphone screeched as it was turned on and Gerald announced it was time to hand your sheets to an opposing team. Zak got up and swapped sheets with an elderly couple and looked down at the answers.

Sitting back down, the conversation returned to the newspaper. "Listen, we are looking at this all wrong. All you have to do is sell adverts and we will fill the rest," said Zak.

Kal was a little confused having earlier sounded a lot more confident. "Fill the rest with what?"

Zak had a way of making things seem possible when they were not. "News. Anything. I don't know. Bullshit. You will figure it out."

It was the kind of vague answers that did not bode well with us at all. Jokes aside, we all knew of how a newspaper worked but we knew little of the inner workings of a newsroom and the process that needed to be followed to publish a copy. It was very much like being asked to run a football club. You know you have to buy some players and put them on the pitch, but there has to be whole load of background tasks that you never see out there on the field.

Gerald proceeded to go through the answers to the quiz. Zak put the sheet in the middle and began marking the answers.

"First of all," said Gerald, "it was of course West End Girls by the Pet Shop Boys."

Zak chuckled to himself.

Akeel glanced across at the old couple. "These budays (old folk) got loads right."

Kal looked into his glass and picked out a piece of orange fragment from the glass with his finger, "Why an Asian newspaper though, Zak?"

It was the perfect opportunity for Zak to share his insight into the industry.

"Because newspapers haven't got a clue about us. They have this idea about us and they stick to it." Zak had never really trusted any other forms of media. "Okay, let me re-phrase that… newsrooms are not bothered about Asians. It is not because they can't write about us, they simply don't know how to."

It was another one of those evaluations that sounded great when said amongst a group of friends who were unlikely to argue to the contrary.

"How many Asian journalists do you know?" He had a point: we knew few Asian journalists but that didn't stop me from trying to prove him wrong.

"I am sure there is. Does Moira Stewart count?"

Zak didn't even dignify my guess with an answer. "There isn't any. The newsrooms are all white and they aren't bothered about hiring us either. It is the whitest profession there is. It doesn't affect them. We aren't the ones buying the newspapers, are we?"

I was sure his analysis had a whole load of flaws but I pretended to know what he was talking about. "Okay fine then. What do we need to do now?"

Gerald said, "And number 6 that was Don't bring me down by ELO."

Zak seemed happy. "Hey the buday (old people) didn't get that one and we did."

"We can set up at the factory. And we need that computer?" said Kal.

"That it?" I asked.

Zak seemed pleased his little speech had worked. "Yeah that is it, for now."

Gerald continued to relay the answers. "And that as you will know was SOS by Abba."

Zak ticked it off. "Oh you got one, Akeel, nice one."

Kal wanted to get things started, straight away. "I think we should try to begin now and aim for an Eid publication. That gives us just over a month."

Zak wanted to get things going fast too. "Yeah but we have to come out before Eid. So that is technically 30 odd days."

Imran didn't look too convinced and neither did I. Despite graduating, Imran now found himself working on a factory floor. New ideas had come and gone. "Four weeks? You want to publish in four weeks?"

"Yes, we set a date and go for it," said Kal. "We got four weeks."

Gerald had reached the end of the quiz. "And the final one was of course, 'Oh Lori' by the Alessi Brothers from 1976. Well done whoever got that one. Let's have a listen to that again as we tally up the scores."

4 PAPERBOY

There was something satisfying about delivering a newspaper. It wasn't the point at which the letterbox was opened but more the whole process leading up to that one defining moment. The route, the bag, the gate, the garden, the fact that I would be reading most of the paper before it arrived at someone's else's door – it helped set the scene for that final stage when the copy was posted through the door. Some days the effort I put in to getting to that blissful period brought me a great deal of pleasure, whilst other days I would see it as it really was – work.

I took up delivering newspapers at the age of 12 after learning my friends had more pocket money than I did. One pal would boast about how his 'unlimited' wealth was due to him being one of the senior paper boys at his local newsagent. He did both the morning and evening rounds. How he must be paid handsomely for his efforts I would recollect.

The first newsagent who employed me was down the road from our house. I had seen a notice in the window several times as I passed and one day decided to walk in and speak to the gentleman sat on a stool behind the counter. The newsagent was named Mr Wilkins and he conducted a short interview asking me my age (which I lied about) and where I lived. Nine of us grew up in a three bedroomed terraced house and despite it being tiny there always seemed to be space. I call it three bedroomed – one was basically a cupboard with a bed in it. My sister had drawn the short straw and slept in a bed in the landing area out in the hallway. No one was allowed into the front room, so it was either the living room, the kitchen or outside. I chose outside.

I stared at him nervously and thought he would most likely decline my 'application' as this job was clearly meant for someone much more accomplished than I.

Surprisingly, he told me come back the next day and said I would be paid £2.20 for the week's round, which to me was a decent amount. A cool £2.20 for working six days a week. This can't take more than twenty minutes, can it? Why have others not taken up this wonderful opportunity to deliver news to their neighbours' doorstep?

The first time I went on the 'round' I was accompanied by Mr Wilkins who made out that he was in fact doing me a favour. Well, why not? I thought. He is paying a reasonable wage for delivering handful of newspapers.

Newsagents, like milkmen, are by their very nature quite practical people. It was most likely due to them being up so early in the morning and they could see the world rush by before others had started their day.

Mr Wilkins had a real sternness about him. He was friendly enough but some days I would hurry into his shop at 7am and see him sat there almost lost in his thoughts, as if asking himself how the decisions he made in life had led him through one turn or another to this one point.

The first day on the job I was presented with the 'best route' and what I should try to avoid, like some unwritten code amongst newspaper deliverers. This, I later learned, turned out to be great advice. At the time I looked up at him and felt, naively I must now admit, I could certainly do a better job than him and in far less time.

A large man, he would struggle at almost every turn and the town of many hills was taking a toll on his frame. Me being younger, quicker and fitter wasn't going to find this at all a problem.

There were a few shortcuts and there were instances where you could deliver two papers by simply leaning over the fence separating the houses.

The first day on the round was scary and I arrived five minutes ahead of time to make sure I had ample opportunity to pack the newspapers. On that day, Mr Wilkins had placed the papers neatly into the bag for me, something he would never again be repeating. I was handed a sheet with addresses and sent on my way.

The paper bag was worn down and was difficult to carry and kept slipping off my shoulders. How Mr Wilkins expected anyone to deliver newspapers with this bag was something I would have to take up with him at a later date, but for now it would do. I couldn't possibly make a complaint on my first day on the job.

As I headed out from the shop, I began to realise something. Maybe this was the reason the small postcard advertising this round had remained there for so long. The round was not easy. I was a skinny kid who never put on weight, no matter how much I ate. It was an in-house family joke and whilst many of my friends tended to be a little bulkier than I was – I just couldn't gain any weight. I never felt it hindered my strength in any way, but this bag was unquestionably too heavy for a kid of my size.

The sack tore into my shoulder but I managed to lessen the pain by switching from left to right every hundred yards.

This was not as easy as many of my friends had made out as there were a whole number of obstacles to avoid. Some of the homes were nearby and I was able to dispense several papers at once. Other times, there was a distance between one house and the next and I would have to walk with most of the bag still full to the next drop. This was probably the worst part of the round as it required me to trek, carrying a heavy load up a steep hill.

This town can sap the energy out of any human and on a crisp morning it can become even more fierce. The hills chip away at your soul, testing your resolve – making young men out of boys. These are the type of inclines that are just as difficult to climb down as they are up. These terraced streets have a wretchedness about them that give you hope, then take it away from you at the same time. People will tell you they understand. They don't.

Then I realised something that taught me very early on that life is indeed cruel and even when you think you know what there is to know it will throw up another surprise. It wants you to imagine things are possible, but in a second all your dreams can be shattered and strewn along the floor for everyone to see. In my case this was Wains Court.

Many of my addresses were grouped together and this I found to be a reasonable enough task. I could deliver most of the round in the first 20 minutes and be back home quite quickly. But then there was Wains Court. Having completed most of the round, this one address was out of the way and the trip would add another ten minutes onto the whole job.

This turned out to be, as I mentioned, a lesson in life. I hated this address with a vengeance as I could not understand why it was included on my round. Why was it here? Had Mr Wilkins put this on the round by mistake? Had this been added on to ensure he was getting value for money out of a small child? I couldn't accept why I was having to do this extra house!

Later, I would try to complete this address first in the hope it would quicken up the job but it did not make a big difference as getting to this address would mean having to haul the full bag of papers with me and then come all the way back to complete the rest of the round. I could see why old Mr Wilkins had left this address to the very end.

I tried to introduce short cuts of my own, but none of these cut any time off my round as they simply didn't work. This was the route and there was nothing you could do about it. I wanted to change it and make it easier, but the route was having none of it and always had the final word.

One week I thought it would be clever to jump over the fences between homes so I wouldn't have to walk all the way to the end of the garden, thus saving me several minutes. A week later Mr Wilkins was notified of my new 'tactic' and told me that one Mrs Jameson had complained after spotting me leaping over her blessed fence. How dare she, I thought! Does she not know the pain I go through to deliver these papers? The sheer pettiness of this woman surprised me. Had she nothing better to do than to peer through her window at this god forsaken time?

Another time I decided to leave the bag at the bottom of a street and then walk up the hill to deliver the papers. This proved to be a master stroke on my part. Until of course I spotted Mr Wilkins driving past. He then went on to explain the importance of keeping the bag on me at all times in case someone was to lift the newspapers.

Even with crime as it is, I could not for one moment imagine anyone wanting to steal a copy of the Mail.

On my return after that first day 'at work' my mother waited at the door to ensure I made it back safely. I was told that this was a bad idea all round and if I didn't like it then there was no shame in just telling Mr Wilkins that I couldn't do it.

You don't know it at the time, but over-protective mothers are the best because it is a quality in others that you very rarely see later in life. As you get older you become detached from these things and no one is there to ask you how you are or worries about you in the same way. As life goes from one crisis to the next you become a bit part player in a grander universe whose job is to worry about everybody else and everything else.

During the days when it rained (and there were many!) it was important to have the bag covered and hid underneath my anorak. When it was cold you had to wear the 'Albert Steptoe' gloves – that way your hands stayed warm and you could still get a firm grip on the paper. Between addresses you could fold newspapers two to three at a time to ensure they were ready to be posted.

I found ways of avoiding dogs by standing perfectly still until the threat was neutralised. Contrary to popular opinion, dogs are not the biggest pitfalls to a paperboy's livelihood. It was in fact badly built letterboxes and gates that simply won't open or shut.

Of the different types of letterboxes, the vertical ones seemed to cause the most amount of nuisance as they were simply not wide enough to accommodate the broadsheets. Others snapped shut and nearly took your hand off. You could also spend valuable time trying to close a broken gate because a common complaint by residents was delivery boys who didn't have the courtesy to close the gate upon their exit.

I praised those homeowners who had decided to place a letterbox at the gate.

The round did get easier as time wore on. After the first few weeks I no longer needed the address sheet, nor did I care if the bag was falling apart. Along the way I would read the latest headlines and how one newspaper would talk about the day's events in a different way to another.

How newspapers reacted to Margaret Thatcher and her government was confusing for me at the time. Some would say they praised her for her strength of character, how she was 'leading this country out of the mess created by the former leaders', whilst others painted her out as an evil individual. Why was there this need to take sides?

I read all the front pages each day and flicked through the interior pages as I walked from address to address. It was my way of filling not only the tedious journey but getting back at my employer. Others were paying for this information – I was getting it for free.

Prison riots, Chernobyl, the Hand of God and the Iran Contra Affair were splashed across the pages during that eventful year. I learnt some people's lives were more important than others.

As the nights drew in and the winter months took hold, the round became more of a monotonous task and my brother's Walkman was my only companion. I must have played Elton John's 'Benny and the Jets' countless times trying to replicate the high notes. In the summer one does not mind getting out of bed and scurrying along to the newsagent. It is, after all, great to be in the rising sun. I wanted to be delivering news to people's homes and hoped they would appreciate my efforts in helping to start their day with a paper.

It is a completely different story in the winter. Our home did not have central heating and simply getting out of bed at 7 o'clock was proving to be more and more tasking as time wore on. I did one day in late November decide it wasn't something I could do that morning. Mr Wilkins will sort it out. I can't be bothered anymore, just let me have an extra thirty minutes in bed. It is windy, wet and cold.

Ten minutes later there was a knock at the door and there was Mr Wilkins.

Mr Wilkins here? At my house? What kind of slave driver was this guy?

My mother told me to get changed and I hurried to the front door.

'In the car, son. Let's go.'

He then drove me from address to address. I guess the job had to be done and there was no way of getting out of it. This was a heavy chain around my neck now and I wasn't going to get out of it by having a lie in or faking an illness.

Neither could I give up having gone against the advice of my mother and wanted to prove to everyone else that I was not a quitter. When things are not going to plan – quitting is not an option. To quit is to fail and to fail is to be tainted for life.

Later in the winter I read about killers on the loose which made me think about my own predicament. It was dark and bitterly cold during those mornings so I decided the night before to ask my sister who was three years older than me to accompany me. She of course was hesitant but was soon cajoled into assisting me by my ever-protective mother.

When the morning came, she was up before I was.

To ensure Mr Wilkins didn't think any less of me I asked her to stand at the end of the street so he couldn't spot her as I couldn't possibly let him know that I was afraid to do the round on my own.

Strangely enough, the round proved to be a lot easier and more enjoyable with two people. I had to, of course, teach her the tricks of the trade.

At first, she wanted only to accompany me to the addresses but soon enough realised that we could cut the time in half if we joined forces. I would like to say that I split the money I got with my sister, but I didn't. She never got paid for anything and remarkably never asked for any payment. Sisters are the best – something you only realise later in life when you have become far too old to even care.

The newspaper round was not easy. It was painful, frustrating and tiring, and it is remembered for being nothing else than those three things.

5 THE SET UP

Ideas are easy. Anybody can come up with an idea and anybody can tell you how to carry out the set of tasks to make that idea work. In theory, everything should pan out the way you think it does. You should be an instant success and people should praise you for having risked everything.

It doesn't happen that way. Nothing happens in the order you thought it might and no one can be confident it will.

First of all, we had all decided we needed a base and somewhere we could call an office. The first few days we had pottered around in front rooms talking about what we needed to do, but it wasn't the same as having a place to meet.

Eventually we decided on the small office in a toilet paper factory. Located in a rundown area of Blackburn, the office and the factory belonged to Khalil's family and his uncles who ran a burgeoning toilet roll business.

However, there was a problem. We could only access the office after 6pm as it was being used during the day by factory staff. This kind of suited us I suppose. With Ramadan kicking in, we were unable to complete any work until the evenings anyway after prayers.

Some things look a lot better during the day than they do at night. The factory was situated at a 'dead end' where the streetlamps had not been fixed for years, so, it was unlikely anyone would be venturing to this part of town after dark.

It was a Tuesday night when we finally met in our 'newsroom'.

Zak was always optimistic. "This isn't too bad."

I was waiting for someone to say something more fitting and Akeel duly obliged: "This place will go down in history as the place where something happened or nothing happened."

He followed that up with something that made even more sense: "Ironic that we are going to be producing shit in a place that produces stuff to wipe the stuff off."

This got more laughs out of everyone including Kal before he looked over at Akeel. "Have you got any better ideas?"

In a way, I was just glad we had somewhere, even if was someone else's office. I had also learnt that one should never take anything for granted and a gesture like this would always be appreciated.

Zak's front room was not a place where you could make plans late into the night. "Hey, I'm happy. Top place. Let's get this shit on the road."

Zak was first to point out what could and could not take place in the office. "No smoking in here then."

Zak and Akeel were not smokers, unlike myself and Kal, but even we knew that toilet rolls and smoking just didn't go together. "No smoking in a paper factory. No excuses. And now I need to relieve myself."

Kal walked out of the room and down the corridor.

We sat around the office looking at each other. The room smelt of paper and there was a lot of dust everywhere covering the walls and the floor.

Minutes later we heard Kal shouting, "Oi."

Akeel got up and hurried down the corridor and returned a minute later.

"What happened?" asked Zak.

"Oh, he ran out of toilet paper."

Kal returned to us minutes later, laughing. "That is not the first time that has happened."

"How can you run out of toilet paper in a toilet roll factory?" said Akeel.

"It is possible. I went to the toilet over there," pointing towards the corridor, "and there were no toilet paper in there. Thankfully, there was a lota (spouted vessel which can be used to wash oneself)."

There were four desks in the office each covered in dust and paper. Kal began clearing one of the tables in the corner and placing all the paper on another desk. Then he paused for a moment and looked around at us all.

He then picked up the paper from that desk and dumped them in the bin. "This shit is old anyway."

I started fiddling with the fax machine in the corner. "This must be really expensive, Kal."

He nodded, throwing more paper into a waste bin.

With no cigarette to occupy my time, I paced around the room picking things and placing them back in their original spot. "Should we come up with a name?"

It was quiet again. There was that smell again wafting in from the factory floor. It was a smell I was very familiar with. It was the smell of manual labour and sweat.

I had worked here once in the summer of 1989. Kal's father encouraged his son to work from an early age. It was probably why he had grown up to be much more business-orientated than the rest of us.

My own father was one of the first Pakistanis to arrive in Lancashire back in the fifties. The story goes he was one of three friends who had docked at Liverpool and decided to make a run for it, escaping to Preston. He spent the next few years working in the mills and then landed a job as a bus conductor and soon enough he was joined by others who had come to the country wanting to make a better life for themselves. He had raised six of us and his nephew who arrived here as a teenager. The word 'cousin brother' is laughed at. But he was our cousin and we treated him as our brother. He, alongside my eldest sibling, Imran and Akeel's father had unselfishly taken on the back breaking jobs to support the wider family. All of us in our group of friends were the sons of the first generation of immigrants who had made the county their home. Our journey seemed almost insignificant compared to theirs, I guess.

In that long hot summer of 1989, I had left school and Kal was spending more and more time at the factory during the day. My father thought it a good idea if I kept him company and at that age you don't mind helping out a friend – but little did I know this was real work.

I awoke at 6.30 in the morning and joined Kal to start the shift at seven. It was a long, hard day. The toilet rolls churned off the end of a conveyor belt and we were both tasked with packing them into bags. They had to be 36 rolls at a time and if you let up for even one moment the machine was unforgiving.

The other workers tended to be newly-wed immigrants and they liked to play classic Mohammed Rafi tunes. Sometimes they liked to join in and sing the chorus out loud. We both found this funny at first but after the same tape had been played ten times it soon became torturous. We knew this type of work was only temporary, but for others who had come to the country hoping for a better life – this was it. They would be working throughout the day and the only joy they would get was the odd sing-along.

At first, it was exciting to be given a level of responsibility. Kal's father, a tall, kind man, always treated me with the level of respect he did for a grown up, which I found endearing. And when we got in trouble, he would always end up reprimanding his own son rather me, even when it was clear it was my fault.

On one occasion, the machine did catch up and had to be switched off until I caught up. This, I learned, was pretty shameful on my part so the floor manager decided it was best if I was put on 'nappy packing' duty.

This turned out to be a lot more accommodating on my part, but there was still a target to be maintained.

At the end of the first week I realised something important. Work is not easy. This was real work, not sitting behind a desk and typing for a living.

Zak made his way to the corner of the room where there was a fridge and small shelf with tea making facilities. "Are we okay using any of these cups?" He picked up a cup and began to clean it with tissue.

Kal nodded as he picked out some files from a desk. "Yeah those are fine."

Zak picked up a further few more utensils. "Have you not got a gora (whitey) cup?"

Kal shook his head. "Why the fuck would we have a gora cup?"

Akeel laughed. "Gora Cup?"

What Zak was referring to was probably the most disgraceful thing ever invented by any person ever. When a builder or a plumber came to the house, the lady of the house would decide it was only polite to make the guy a cup of tea. But rather than make it in a cup which was used by the rest of us, one had to use the 'Gora Cup'. Basically, the cup was a separate container all together and one which was offensive both in name and in purpose.

Zak laughed. "I'm joking. If you had a gora cup here I would be worried." We both frowned at Zak who liked to point out our inconsistencies whenever he could. "Come on. You know you all had one at home. There is no point trying to be all nice about it now."

Akeel still looked a little confused. I always found it a little strange that whilst Akeel had spent much of his childhood in Pakistan, he was unaware of such levels of closet racism within our own community from those of us who had spent our formative years growing up here. Probably a good thing, I always thought, to be shielded from these things.

I paced around the office and sat down, putting my feet up on a desk. Kal peered up from his drawer. I took my feet off the desk.

"Okay, we should come up with a name then," said Zak.

This was not going to be easy. A name.

"It's all about what we are," added Zak.

"We want to portray a certain image, don't we." I disliked these brainstorming sessions as they could drag on.

"Yes. Image," said Zak.

Akeel stood up as if that might help him come up with a great idea. "Some Image."

Kal turned his head. "Asian Image."

Zak raised his hand and added, "All for Asian Image, put your hands up."

We all raised our hands. Akeel looked across at us and raised both hands. "That was easy. I thought that would be the hardest part."

"The hardest part is convincing people that you are a newspaper," said Zak. "And not another bunch of fly-by-night wannabe guys."

Kal smiled. "It was easy, Zak."

I was more pessimistic. "But we are a bunch of fly-by-night wannabe guys."

6 A GAME YOU MUST PLAY

We left the council building and stood on the steps outside and lit a cigarette each. It was freezing again and the town centre was eerily quiet and dark; thankfully, the scarf I had 'borrowed' earlier from my brother was coming in handy.

"What a waste of time that was," I said flicking the ash over a railing.

Kal had joined me at a meeting with a council officer which had turned out to be a little less useful than we had thought. After being quite confident on the phone, the council officer for all good intentions had invited one of his Asian colleagues to the meeting. This was the second time this had happened to us. We had arranged a meeting with a council official and for some reason he had invited in one of his Asian colleagues who had immediately taken a disliking to us.

The meeting, which I did sense we were lucky to get, gave us little time to explain what we were doing and became more about us having to convince the 'Asian go-between'.

We began a slow walk back to the car. "You know why they do that, don't you, Kal?"

"Why?"

"It is all about making us feel welcome. I think it's nice."

"Bollocks," said Kal. "You don't haul out the resident paraplegic when you hold a meeting with someone who is visually impaired, do you? They just want to make out they know one of us."

I would have laughed if I could be bothered and wasn't so disheartened. It is one thing being friends with someone and it is another thing going into business with a friend. It was the first meeting we had been to together and it had not gone to plan.

"And another thing," added Kal. "You see this is a common mistake many organisations make – they compare us all to their own 'Asian'. Like this guy is probably a nice chap, but in his role is going to pretend he knows what is the best for the rest of us. He has made it and doesn't want the rest of us to spoil the party."

We had another meeting lined up; maybe we would have better luck there, but it wasn't for a few hours later that evening.

'You Better You Bet', by The Who played on the radio as we headed out to speak to someone who was meant to be a local 'godfather'. We had heard some names being mentioned and decided it might be an idea to go and see them and if they could help us.

Kal was driving. The red Mazda was a cross between a sportscar and a family car, with headlights that flipped open.

"So, who is this guy then?"

"Some guy."

Whenever we went anywhere we rarely made pointless conversation. He in particular tended to save that for an audience.

"What guy?"

"Apparently he knows people and might be able to help us. May be able to get us some contacts. He is well in with some people."

We entered a long driveway and then a garden area, parking up alongside several expensive vehicles. Neither of us were impressed by gimmicks and wealth. It was one of the things that annoyed us as those with a 'bit of money' tended to be a big disappointment.

Opening the door was a well-dressed gentleman who greeted us with the customary 'Salaams'. We removed our shoes – which I never had a problem with, but could sense some worry when I looked over at Kal. He was self-conscious of the odour that may emanate from his feet. Eventually he took off his shoes and our host led us to his large sitting room area complete with Chesterfield sofas and hideous large mirrors. I could never really trust anyone who had a lot of mirrors in the house.

I felt I should be the first to speak. "Thank you for seeing us, uncle." Through habit we would call anyone older than us 'uncle' as a mark of respect. There was this need for some people to perpetuate familiar stereotypes of Asian elders. The reality I'm afraid is different.

Mr Irfan was of medium build with a mosque hat on and was constantly cleaning his nose with a handkerchief. "Khalil, your father doing well?"

"Yes, he gives his salaam. He is back from Pakistan now."

He got straight to the point: "All is good then. So how can I help you both?"

Kal decided to roll off the customary introduction, "Well, we are setting up a newspaper and we thought it might be good to get your support. You could maybe point us the right direction?"

"I see. A newspaper. An Asian newspaper you said on the phone earlier?"

"Yes, free for all the houses in Blackburn," I said.

He paused. A teenager entered the room with some tea and biscuits.

Mr Irfan gestured to us both to help ourselves and began to pour the tea. "Good idea. How are you going to compete with the LET?"

The LET, as people referred to it, was our local daily newspaper, the Lancashire Evening Telegraph.

"We have no intention to," said, Kal. "They do their thing and we do ours. We just think there is a market for an Asian newspaper. The thing we need at this stage is adverts."

"Money from me."

"No, not you. Could you help to get us into the council and some of the main business people?"

"I could make some calls and some introductions if that helps."

I nodded my head as if to show my appreciation. "That would be good enough."

But there seemed to be a catch.

Mr Irfan leaned back in his chair. "Why don't you start – and I don't want to tell you what to do – by doing a feature on someone who has been helping the community for many years. Someone who has a real link with people."

Kal glanced at me and back at Mr Irfan. "Who?"

"Well, me? You know I don't like to talk about myself and I just want to remain humble. I just do it to help. I established two community groups and am setting up a new one. And was recently made chairman."

Kal did like to praise others. "Chairman. Congratulations. How many members of this new group?"

"At the moment there are five of us."

I nodded again to show I was impressed. "Five people?"

"I am chairman. Mama Ranzeeb is the Vice chairman. Younis Bhai is treasurer, Barlas is the Secretary and Cha Cha (uncle) Mian is the honorary president."

"So, everyone in the group has a role?" asked Kal.

He seemed surprised that he had been asked this question. "Yes, otherwise they wouldn't be members, would they?"

Actually, in a strange way that made sense.

It seemed we would have to congratulate people even if it was a means to an end.

Kal heaped more praise on Mr Irfan. "Okay, I can see why that would work. You must be very proud. What do you actually do?"

This was more like it. Praise the host and he is bound to give us a hand. "We help people. Our community. This is the third group and I am also chairman of the other two groups."

But then Kal began to tire of this self-congratulatory attitude. "Yes, you said that."

Mr Irfan continued, "We are doing a dinner for the community and will be hosting the Pakistani counsel general. In some weeks.

It will be good to report from there. But first an interview with me would get people talking."

Few things impressed me less than people who admired themselves. But it was important to be polite and courteous to everyone. "I see. Interesting. Okay, we can let you know."

Suddenly I could sense Mr Irfan's warm and welcoming attitude drain from his face as he attempted to reassert some authority. Growing up, we were taught to speak to our elders in a certain way and once you said something disrespectful, and in my case without knowing it, there was no going back.

I guess it wasn't the answer Mr Irfan had been expecting. "Let me know? I don't give this opportunity to many people. I can ring the Telegraph and they will do the interview straight away. I know you guys so I thought I would help you. This is an exclusive for you and you should be glad I am offering this to you."

Kal interjected, "I am sure you will. Like Shuiab said, we can let you know."

I felt Mr Irfan had been waiting for an opportunity to tell us what he really thought. "Let me explain something – in this game you will need to be a bit smarter, young fellows. This is a game you must both play. If you don't do favours no one will take you seriously and you might find that people will close doors in your faces. You scratch my back and I will scratch yours – you know how the saying goes."

When you have nothing to offer you tend to put up with certain ideas and thought processes.

But Kal didn't have the patience and once someone had crossed a particular line he felt it his duty to speak his mind. "It seems at this stage we are the ones who are scratching more backs and putting some thehl (oil) on there too!"

I chuckled and then saw Mr Irfan's expression change. "Khalil, I had thought you might have more sense in you. In this town there are some people who can easily stop you doing anything. It is a small town and we have many gorays (white folk) who look up to us and support us. Without us nothing gets done. The gorays don't want the hassle of issues they don't understand so they trust us to make sure things get done. At the moment you are nothing."

"You make it sound like Imperial India," I said.

Mr Irfan cleaned his right ear and then looked at the contents. "Everyone needs to know their place, that's all. You two have been away, haven't you? You think you are so special because you went away and came back?"

We both sat there silently.

"Blackburn is not some backward town that needs rescuing."

Kal attempted to calm matters down having indirectly stoked them up in the first place. "We didn't mean to be disrespectful in any way, uncle, but we just came to ask if you could help us a bit. We will look at doing the interview; let us first get going."

By this stage Mr Irfan had lost all interest. "Well then." And got up from his seat as if to say he had had enough of our petty little stories and wanted us to leave. I had never been to any household where the host had got up from his seat as it could be deemed as an extremely rude gesture. You just didn't do it; but I felt it was just his way of showing who was in charge.

"Well then," said Kal.

"Okay then," I added.

Mr Irfan cleaned his nose again. "I am busy and have many things to do. Do let me know about the interview."

7 CUSTARD CREAMS

Leaving Mr Irfan was a bit of a disappointment. People who you think may help out tend to wait until you are of some importance or value before they stick their name to the banner.

That is not to say we had not met people who wanted to assist us in this venture and ask nothing in return. But at the very beginning, those types of people tend to be few and far between.

We both returned to the car. "Well, what do you make of that?"

It began to rain and Kal turned on the windscreen wipers.

He was not in the mood to dress up this 'meeting'. "Waste of time. He basically wanted a free article to tell everyone how important he is."

"So why did we go and see him?"

"To give him a chance. Then he can't say we never went to see him. A lot of these people are like that. They want to be visited by anyone doing anything new so they can tell other people that we came to see them. It's all bullshit."

The worst part of the day was going back to the others and telling them the individual who we were told was of some significance was in fact the same as the rest.

I skipped through the radio stations and pushed in a Snap tape we couldn't get enough of. "Why did you congratulate him becoming a chairman of a group that does fuck all?"

He had always done this to people as a way of making the other person feel at ease. "Look, we both know this guy is not going to help us. We must do it ourselves and make our own contacts. Nobody cares anymore about who and what you are. All that shit is gone."

I sighed. "I think he wanted us to massage his ego." The rain shower had passed and the wipers were making a screeching sound. "You can turn off the wipers now." Kal did so.

He always had a way of making things seem a lot more positive than they were by being brutally honest about the situation. "He wanted us to bend over so he could shaft us and at the end of the session wanted us to thank him for doing so. 'It's all a game.' There's no game. There's no 'special goray' who will only speak to him. All that shit he said in there was to make us scared and think that we need him."

It began to rain again. "You should put the wipers back on." Kal promptly put the wipers back on.

I had to make out that I agreed with his sentiments. "I was hoping it would it be lot easier than this. We go see some 'godfather type', he gives us some adverts and we print a newspaper."

Kal searched around for the lighter in his car, something he always did before realising he had lost it months ago. I handed him a lighter I had been fidgeting with.

He lit a cigarette as did I. "Do you think these people really care about the likes of us? He doesn't give a shit about people like us! We are just a stepping-stone to their next pointless title. They don't want us to succeed because it will prove the whole system is not rigged. And the reason it is like this is because we have pricks like this in charge."

I laughed. "Don't you know he's a chairman."

This seemed to incense Kal further. "Chairman of what? Chairman of a bullshit group that is there to make out he is doing something."

It stopped raining again and the wipers began to make a screeching sound again. "Turn them off now."

"Will you shut the hell up about the wipers. Leave them on."

"I hate that sound. It pisses me off. Just turn them off now."

Kal sighed again and puffed on his cigarette, blowing the smoke in my direction and purposely waited for the sound to become unbearable before switching off the wipers.

There was a momentary silence and then I pointed out what really mattered to me during the visit. "I mean, he gave us custard creams."

"What?" Kal had a confused look on his face.

"Custard creams. You know when you aren't that welcome when they serve you custard creams. It was disrespectful and just damn rude. I hate the bastard biscuits."

There was silence as we puffed on our cigarettes through the small gaps in the windows.

Kal finally got round to asking, "What would you have rather got?"

"Jaffa Cakes. They serve Jaffa Cakes, you know the guy wants to impress you. Serving custard creams to another human being is very much like going to his wedding in your pyjamas – you do it to take the piss out of the host."

"You really hate them biscuits."

"Don't you?" I asked curiously

"Well, yeah… I don't know… I like to split them and lick out the middle."

"That's the most disgusting thing I have ever heard. That's nearly as bad as meeting a woman who says 'Yaar' (friend) at the end of everything."

Kal didn't answer. He had gotten used to my little annoyances in life and continued to flick cigarette ash out of the window back on to his leather jacket.

"I hate the whole yaar thing," I added. "It is bad enough when you meet a bloke who says it but a woman saying it is a big turn off for me. 'Don't be boring yaar.' 'Come on yaar', 'You are such a joker.. yaaaar'."

Kal chuckled.

"Next time we go anywhere and if the bastard puts custard creams in front of us, we are walking."

Kal nodded.

8 OUR TOWN

Everybody loves the town they grew up in. Whenever someone speaks ill of it, we defend it for all that it is worth, and we hope that others will view it with the same way we see it. But what if your town is shit? Sorry, but this is exactly how some people felt. The town of Blackburn was for all purposes not the greatest place on the planet. This had nothing to do with the people who were lovely and warm, but the town itself. It was just not that good.

When you are a child you see things differently because your friends and family make up that period of your life. People who are now dead were alive. We went to school, we went to mosque in the evenings and we spent the rest of the time playing football or cricket in the back alleys surrounding our homes. The summers and the winters merged into this one whole season and all that mattered was the odd wedding, some funerals and people coming to sit in your front room to smoke Embassy reds.

As you grow older, you realise the town is shit. And if that wasn't enough, the surrounding towns are shit too. People were just getting by and trying their best in miserable weather and low wages. Yet, if any 'outsider' said this, we would get so angry.

We had a good football team that had put us on the map, but barring that, there was very little else going on. If it wasn't for the football, Kenny Dalglish and Alan Shearer, there is no idea what we would do to pass our days. It was a great time to be alive if you were a Blackburn Rovers supporter as you could stick two fingers up at the likes of Manchester United, Liverpool and Arsenal, who felt we were pissing on their patch. We were the best. Thank god for Jack Walker. Yet, the wonderful football masked our actual misery.

We were a footballing family and my eldest brother attended his first match aged only 11 in 1966 alongside a neighbour named Roy. His love for the club continued and through the seventies he was branching out to away matches, even venturing to Turf Moor. That was not a time to be brown on the terraces, but somehow he did it and had a scar on his face to show for his unwavering support of the blue and whites. My other older two brothers followed in his footsteps, and soon enough I joined them on the terraces in 1985 with my first match – a 3-0 defeat at home to Barnsley. On one occasion I was with my second eldest brother, who was about 20 at the time, and we had been stood on the back step of the terraces at the Darwen End and a man who was clearly intoxicated had put both his hands on my brother's shoulders. My heart froze. It was fight time and I wasn't even ready. He then paused and politely asked my brother to move aside as he needed to urinate on the back wall.

There was a joke between us. Those who 'picked-up' football in the nineties had no idea what the 'real fans' had to endure on those cold winter nights watching drab second division mid-table games.

The past five years was about all-seater stadiums, fancy half-time shows and live football - not standing on the terraces hoping the opposition didn't have a black player. Those monkey chants would cut through the soul and I was only on the side lines helplessly watching it happen.

Some opposition fans sang out that we were 'a town full of Pakis' when they visited but by the early nineties we were chanting 'loadsa loadsa money' in response.

But that was the football and not the town itself.

It was no surprise the first thing anyone did when they had the chance was leave and only return to watch the football. But we had a saying which I will try my best to translate from Punjabi: 'Wherever the donkey wanders it soon finds its way home.'

The only thing that makes anyone come back to home, to the town of their childhood, is family and necessity. This was a case of both.

I had run out of places to go and settled back home in late 1997, with no money and an overdraft.

Coming back here meant you had failed. It meant you had tried your luck elsewhere and couldn't pull it off so you had to return to the place of your birth because that is the only place that would accept you for who you were. For a while at least you feel like an outsider and stranger trying to fit back in.

The town itself was a mish mash of people and roads. It is unusually hilly. These are, as we like to refer to them, 'proper hills', not slight inclines that others thought were steep elsewhere in the country.

The Asians stayed in their patch and the white folk in theirs.

Football and the town centre brought us all together in a shared experience, but it was not always joyous.

We knew people looked down upon us and thought we were stuck in the seventies. The word 'backward' was banded about quite regularly, but much of this was just a way of making them feel more supercilious. There was nothing backward about Blackburn.

I recollected showing one patronizing Londoner around town and he seemed genuinely surprised to see a McDonald's here.

What I could never understand was how our friends from London would make the trip up the M6 and pretend they were far superior than us, then immediately head to the three-day market to see if they could grab a bargain before travelling home.

We had two markets – an indoor one which, despite having the odd highlight was boring as hell, and an outdoor market which had some of the best stalls around. It was great during the summer I guess but that market had to be one of the most miserable places to frequent when the temperature dropped.

If something happened 'up here' it didn't really matter. We existed in this bubble from the outside world. Small northern towns had been left behind by successive governments to fend for themselves and we just got on with it.

You could spend your life playing cricket, watching football or driving along Whalley Range in a brown Toyota Starlet, which we did thanks to my cousin, and time would pass you by.

It wasn't just about Asians. None of this was. It wasn't about brown or white. Rich or poor or who was to blame for what. We were all facing the same shit every day together.

We didn't want to make any changes. We were not here to save this place from going to the dogs. We just wanted to make a few quid and have a laugh, trying to publish a paper in our home town but things don't always turn out the way you think.

9 THIS IS DICKENS STREET NOT FLEET STREET

Everyone knows that one friend whom they attempt to shield from other people. Not that they are embarrassed of him in any way, but he is unlikely to give you a glowing reference when you make that introduction. Rather than begin the conversation with the usual pleasantries this person will more than likely ask, 'How do you now this twat?'

Benny was that person.

A man who didn't like to say what you wanted to hear and in all honesty didn't care. Of course we wanted to give him a chance, but he was likely to forget that you ever forgave him the last time on the next occasion your paths crossed.

Our temporary office was attracting attention and in a very short time was being frequented by other 'friends' who thought they had a right to be there.

Amongst them was Benny who paid us a visit one Friday evening.

Zak looked up from him screen. "Hey, what are you doing here?"

A Pakistani man of small height with thick hair and moustache, he would wear trousers, a shirt and a colourful tie almost daily – even at weekends. When he turned up to play football, the shirt and trousers stayed on, only the footwear changed.

Benny had in recent years been compared to Begbie from the movie *Trainspotting*, both in looks and attitude. Once whilst stood in a takeaway waiting for his meal, a customer had entered and greeted him, 'Alright pal". Benny being, well, Benny, had replied, "I'm not your fucking pal." A fight broke out and two other customers having entered the establishment had become immediately concerned for the welfare of the smaller fellow who was being picked on by the larger gentleman. Benny had lit a cigarette, stood back and watched the ensuing mayhem, oblivious to the carnage he had caused.

Despite being a few years older than me he behaved like someone well beyond his years and could well find himself conversing with the fifty-somethings and ordering them about during weddings and funerals. He glanced over at Akeel who was sat in the corner trying to find some errors on a sheet of paper. Then like a bad review he began as he meant to go on. "I just thought I would pop by to see what you saddos are doing in my town."

It was a familiar opening statement from a man who thought he 'owned' vast areas of the town through the connections he had made over the years. He knew everyone and everyone knew him, and whilst his crude behaviour could come across as quite aggressive, he was someone with a level of honesty and loyalty in him.

If he had ever decided to stand as a local councillor he most certainly would have won every election by a landslide, because people feared he knew too much about them or simply could not say no to someone who had come to their rescue when they needed him most.

The truth was much of this was bravado, but it was a pleasure to watch. The problem was we were about to be on the other end of his little lesson in life.

"Your town?" I asked.

"Yeah, as you know, I own this town. What, you think you can just come here and tell us what to do? You guys think you are better than us? Nothing happens without me knowing."

The idea that he knew things that others did not was also a common theme to many of his conversations and it almost certainly gave him a presence in any room and raised expectations with anyone he ever met. He sat down on the edge of a desk and folded his arms, giving the impression he was about to lecture a class of secondary school students.

Whilst some of us were happy enough to humour this show of strength, Kal never really did warm to his conversation. "You own shit. In fact, shit owns more than you."

It was all Benny needed to begin his analysis of the newspaper industry. "I can make things very difficult for you lads, so behave yourselves. You do know what I am capable of? It is easy being a big fish in a small town, but may I remind you that I am a shark – a shark with balls."

Kal laughed out loud. "A shark doesn't have balls."

"This one does!" Benny smiled back stroking his moustache with both fingers. "So, this newspaper? It will never work."

"Why not?" I asked. This time, hoping he would say something more earnest.

Sadly, he didn't. "Half the town can't read and the other half are too busy in Tesco's trying to get their buy one get one free shit."

"It's Tesco," Zak said.

"What?"

"You said Tesco's. It's not Tesco's or Asda's. There is no 'S' at the end of the words," pointed out Zak.

"Okay, Tesco!" emphasised Benny. "Dickhead."

After our encouraging start, Kal was not about to let this guy put a downer on things again. "You see it's people like you that like to take a negative angle on everything. You need to be more positive about this town. We could be the New York of the north one day."

"Come on," said an incensed Benny. "And here we are sat in Central Perk. And this guy (pointing at me sarcastically) is Chandler and you can be Joey. And Aki can be Rachel. Knobhead."

Zak laughed and then thought it best not to draw attention to himself.

"The only way you will be successful is if you print hard hitting investigative articles. Not this namby pamby crap," added Benny, realising he had hit a raw nerve.

"Namby pamby is such an underrated term," I responded.

He got up from the desk and paced around the room, stroking his moustache before sitting down again. "I give you two months. If you want my advice, I think you should hire some proper goray journalists who know what they are doing."

'Goray' was a common term used by many Asians growing up in

the seventies and eighties. It referred to white people.

Kal was still having none of it. "Just leave, you add nothing to the debate."

And then like they always did, things took a turn for the worse, "I am trying to help you guys. No one is going to take you pricks seriously. This fucker (pointing at me) has got three GCSEs."

"I have five actually and a degree in politics," I said almost apologetically.

"It isn't worth shit. Degree in politics? You might as well have graduated in cock sucking. You think you are qualified to run a newspaper? Your English is so bad I am surprised you can sign your own name."

He laughed at his own joke and before anyone could reply he added, "You know, let me tell you all a story. I met this uncle last week after a long time and he said 'Aslamulaikum' and I said 'Waalaikumussalam' and we shook hands… we had not met since his son got married…"

I frowned. "Why must you do that?"

"Do what?"

"Why must you set the scene?"

"But I did say 'Aslamulaikum' and he did say 'Waalaikumussalam'."

Benny hated being interrupted and stared at me, stroked his moustache again as Akeel smiled. "And we started talking and he said he had been living here for thirty years and met a lot of people and knew this town better than anyone else. He used to work in a factory, much like this one but a little bit bigger and he realised one important thing that would help race relations for the modern era. He used to have white friends, one black friend and two Hindus on his shift and every day they would talk about everything."

An impatient Kal scratched his head. "Come on."

Benny was getting frustrated. "Shut the fuck up."

"What he told me was simple. He said this town is full of three types of people. The goray, the apnay (us) and the dickheads. The only people worth anything and mixing with one another are the dickheads."

After such a build-up it was the type of deep meaningful analysis that we had come to expect from Benny, or in this case the 'uncle' he had met.

Unusually, Kal decided to give him one more chance. "That was your grand story? You got us all turned on for that? You still haven't told us why did you came here?"

"To make sure you don't embarrass us all," exclaimed Benny, standing up from the desk.

"What's your point?" added Zak.

Benny began pacing around the room again.

"People don't like me for stating the obvious. My point is you should just do as I say, or you are preparing yourself for one big fall."

"Okay, what's that?" added Zak, knowing full well he was inviting more abuse.

It had taken him a while but he was finally going to tell us what he really wanted to say. We were simply not good enough. "British values. Be proud to be Brits. This great country has given us everything – we should give back to them. It is time we stopped talking about Pakistan or Bangladesh and celebrated this wonderful country of ours. The country of our birth. You know, Thatcher, Churchill and Oasis."

Kal was beginning to tire of him. "Evolution was not kind to you, was it. What is that going to achieve?"

Whilst we had all in our all way been content to be British, we were unlikely to boast about it every opportunity. It hadn't occurred to us that to be British we had to tell others how British we were.

Benny, on the other hand, loved to call out anyone who was not praising this 'blessed country'.

If you didn't support England at both football and cricket you were the reason there was so much racism in some parts of society. It was up to you to change, not for the country to be more accommodating. If you behaved more patriotically then people would not look down upon you so much. If you stayed out of trouble and kept your head down the host community would leave you alone as they may well decide to send you all back where you came from if you didn't play ball.

Benny in his rudimentary approach to things was about to explain how we could find a way out of our predicament but it would mean us having to make one major sacrifice. "Okay this paper is only going to run if you get adverts. Is that correct?"

I nodded and Zak sighed. "So, the way I see it the more goray (white) arses you lick, the more adverts you will get. Goray love it when you lick their arses."

"Are we talking about the same thing here?" asked Zak.

Being subservient was a means to an end in the big wide world and whilst we might think we know what it takes to step up the career ladder, we knew very little.

Benny responded to that 'joke' by laying into what was left of our self-esteem. "Fuck you. You have to write about the issues that we are facing but hire some gora to do it for you. Use your heads. Nobody is going to take you guys seriously. Like I said, you aren't proper journalists. You are going to shame what is a wonderful profession with a great history. Proper journalists don't sit around in bog roll factories at night typing on one computer. This is Dickens Street not Fleet Street."

Even I was impressed he managed to make those rhyme.

Kal continued, now in vain, to challenge Benny. "What the hell is wrong with you? We don't need qualifications to do this. We can do it ourselves."

That wasn't entirely true though.

We knew we were not 'proper' journalists and, barring Zak who had a media qualification to his name and was editor of his university newspaper, we really had no idea what a newsroom did. This glaring fact had occurred to us on several occasions already, but it just seemed to be a lot harsher when someone else said it. Even if that someone was Benny.

"Deep down you all know that I am right. Without proper educated professionals this whole set up of yours won't work. You need to earn some respect for yourselves. Why do we need an Asian paper anyway – we got our local rag? You lot are just segregating."

Benny did like to switch from one subject to the next without hesitation as it meant he never actually lost an argument. It was a tactic that had stood him in good stead through the years. When you are likely to get into any discussion which requires you to listen to another opinion, switch between subjects and hope no one notices.

Zak had now stopped working completely. "What the dickheads from the other dickheads?"

Towns like Blackburn had issues with segregation, but this was something that may not seem clear to someone who resided in the town. I mean, who is to say you are segregated if you have not known anything else?

We had lived here for most of our lives, albeit the previous seven years, when we had been at university and elsewhere, and segregation was not something that really affected us. It hadn't made a huge difference to our lives.

"Yes, now you're all getting it. You lot are just making us all out to be different when we are all the same. Me, you, the 'dickheads'. We knock back jugs of lassi (Traditional South Asian drink) and they drink pints of beer. In the end it all comes out the same way when we piss it out in the bush," pointed out Benny.

"You piss in the bush?" said Kal, now having resigned to making jokes to shut Benny down.

"Laugh all you want but why do you think white folk move out when one of us moves in?"

Everyone shook their heads. "I am sure you are going to enlighten us with your local study of demography and sociology," said Zak.

Benny sat and moved back into the centre of the room. "They

move out because you guys fuck the place up when you move in."

Kal was indignant. "Come on Benny, that's low even for you."

Undeterred Benny continued, "Okay tell me this. Asian family moves in. Then another Asian family moves in and then white family moves out. Soon enough the whole street is Asian. What happens then?" He didn't wait for an answer. "The rest of us Asians hate the fact the whole fucking street is Asian. Even we know it's shit and can't wait to get another house in a predominantly white area. Problem is then white family moves out and the whole process starts again."

Zak shook his head again. "Why don't the white folk stay then?"

Benny laughed again mockingly. "Because you bastards keep knocking on the doors asking them if they want to sell their house."

Kal had seriously had enough. "You can't blame one set of people for another set of people wanting to move out. You make us sound like some sort of vermin."

Benny laughed out loud. "Would you want to see this pisshead every morning?" pointing at me.

This was typical of Benny. I think he enjoyed riling us up and a part of me felt he did it on purpose. "The sooner people like you and those around you realise that this country has given you so much, the better it will be for the rest of us."

With that he began to make himself a cup of tea in the corner. "Fucking inbreds, the lot of you."

It was worrying hearing such things being said by someone who we thought was on 'our side', yet Benny was happy enough to make these suggestions without a second thought.

Akeel was incensed. "It is people like you coming out with shit like that which makes it difficult for the rest of us. How the hell do you expect anyone else to behave towards us if our own are talking bullshit like that?"

Few things ever fazed Benny and he turned and sipped his tea. "You'll live."

I would also be lying if at this stage I didn't admit I was becoming a little anxious with the whole newspaper launch idea he had mentioned. Maybe Benny was right. Maybe we were just kidding ourselves and journalism and publishing should in fact be left to the professionals. To be a journalist requires a level of qualification and we knew nothing about this.

It was time we all admitted some home truths and I got up and put my arm around Benny.

"Oh brother Benny, if I may be kind enough to call you by your correct title, let me explain some things to you. We haven't got a penny to our name. We haven't got a fucking clue what to write. And we are not coming back to take over the town. We just want to print a bastard newspaper and get some bastard adverts. Check out this sad excuse for an Englishman." I pointed towards Kal who now had his feet resting on a desk.

"Up until last week he thought newspapers were printed on those old presses from the cowboy movies." I turned to Zak. "Why this guy comes out every day wearing a three-piece suit I have no idea." And then we both swivelled to look at Akeel. "And this bloke. Well, He's a wonderful human being... and... well... you know." Akeel nodded in agreement.

"Look around you. Look at where we are. Do you think we care about failing? And more importantly we don't even know which arse to lick."

The idea of sucking up to someone to get by was demeaning.

Kal joked, "We aren't licking no gora arse."

"Nope. No way. We do NOT lick arses," added Zak, emphasising the 'not'.

Akeel had until this stage not said a word. "Never. Gorays should be licking OUR arses."

So widespread had the use of the term gora become that people tended to forget what it meant so I decided to remind them again, "And can we stop using the word gora. It means 'whitey'. It's pretty racist."

Benny decided to pipe up again. "No it isn't – we use it in a loving way. You know that 'gora', there be's a gora there, the gora made me do it and so on so forth. I am pretty sure the goray are alright with us using it. They know their place and we know ours."

Something we all knew wasn't true, but everyone loves to try to justify their prejudices. I wasn't impressed. "We hardly use it lovingly. We use it to take the piss. Next time just call him a 'whitey' to his face and be done with it."

It brought out laughs in everyone before Kal, mimicking a southern Texas accent, said, "Now, why would we do that, my dear fellow, that would be just so damn rude."

10 RUSTAM

We slowed behind some vehicles heading into the town centre. "Hey, there's Rasputin." I pointed to a tall, slim man with a long brown coat and shalwar kameez (Asian style trousers and top) strutting along the pavement beside me.

Kal squinted slightly as it was dark and difficult to make out the face. "Are you sure that's him?"

Rasputin had got his name after we had spotted him in a club several years earlier. He was stood on the side of the dance floor for what seemed like ages in his sky blue shalwar kameez. It was, of course, an unusual sight to see a man wearing the traditional South Asian clothing and slippers in a club of all places, but there he was. At the time I seemed to be more surprised that others in the club were not taken aback by a man wearing a blue shalwar kameez with a long black beard standing motionless. Every so often clubbers would push past him but he seemed oblivious to what was going on around him.

What happened next would help to rename him the Mad Monk. As anyone who has heard the track Rasputin by Boney M will know, the introduction is a little longer than normal and as the music played our mysterious clubber took to the dancefloor.

We both looked around to see if this was like some sort of joke and we were being filmed for some hidden camera show. But no. A small crowd developed around him as he swivelled and skipped across the floor in his blue shalwar kameez and for a moment even took hold of his nara (small rope which holds up the pants) and swung it around in front of him.

Many would have been embarrassed to see such a sight, but I think we were enthralled more than anything else. Rasputin danced to the whole track barefoot and he was truly magnificent.

"Yeah, that's definitely him." I pulled down the window. "Has to be him. What's he doing here? We should stop and chat to him."

"And what?" Kal lit up another cigarette. "Ask him if he still frequents clubs to disco dance?"

Having never met or spoken to 'Rasputin' I probably would have more respect for him than the man we were about to meet.

We pulled into the town centre and parked up.

"What's this appointment I need to go to?" asked Kal, who today had wrapped up half his face with a scarf. And it was no wonder – today was a particularly nippy day. There is cold and then there is 'boring cold', I always thought. In the movies people tend to be in some sort of 'exciting cold' but here in Blackburn it was 'boring cold'. You know it is just cold for the sake of being cold and there is absolutely no way you could make it exciting.

I had got told some wedding company wanted to have a meeting with us. There was one drawback though, the meeting had been arranged by Rustam who was in all respects a serial womaniser.

Rustam had a real sense of bravado about him. When it came to women, he could be the most brazenly sexist person you could meet. He liked to talk about women as nothing more than sex objects.

Having learned that we were about to publish a newspaper he wanted to pay us a visit with a 'friend' of his. We decided it best not to meet at the toilet factory so as not to come across as… well… cheap and opted instead to meet at a town centre coffee shop.

Men like to comment on women a lot. We like to think that we know what is best for them. The way they dress, how they should behave and what they should read. We know best – or we think we do.

But things were changing, and many young men were already being left behind. Girl power clashed with lad culture and the result was a great deal of confusion, especially if you were a young Asian man.

Rustam was not a great looking guy if I am going to be honest, but he seemed to think he was very good with women. It was all about portraying oneself to be more important than one was.

He had slicked back hair, a beard and an earring. He had the right car, the right outfits and the most importantly the right story to tell. It was all about selling a false narrative about himself. Now, I am not going to lie. We had all gone through that phase where we wanted people to think we were 'cool'. But I certainly wasn't, because I used the word 'cool' far too often.

Rustam walked in wearing a designer leather jacket and velvet slip on shoes. You know you are special when you have a set of velvet slip on shoes with the gold medallion on the front. It really finishes off the look.

Kal and I were sat having ordered two cups of breakfast tea that came in a metal pot along with some apple pie.

"How's it going, boys?"

"Yeah all is good." I nodded.

"Oh, paper da daso... So, tell me about this paper of yours?"

Rustam had a habit of saying something in Punjabi and then translating it into English in the same sentence. At first it was funny but after the hundredth time it was probably one of his most annoying aspects.

Kal had already decided this was going to be a bad meeting but we had little else to do that day and Rustam could be quite insistent. "We told you before, Rustam. You know what it is about. It is an Asian newspaper and we are distributing it to people's homes."

"Achah (okay), that's good that's good."

Meeting him for the first time you would think he was the most connected person in town. But it was all an act.

The thing about Rustam was, he basically wanted to impress a woman he knew and he wanted to use us to do it, so I could sense this was not going to be a very pleasant meeting. People use the word 'pervert' to describe men like Rustam. I would disagree. Perverts tend not to put so much effort into being perverted. If there were qualifications for perversion, Rustam would have graduated a long time ago. He was something else and lived up to his nickname Chuppah Rustam (A dark horse), a common Asian phrase to describe someone who would work undercover.

To him it was also all about favours and links. He liked to make out that he had an endless amount of contacts that may benefit you. When a woman was involved his brain would go into overdrive like some super-computer linking one person's skills and needs with another. Eventually, there was a purpose to him and by using one person he could then use the other.

"Okay, lads, this bird she is proper into me so just play along."

This normally meant that we should pretend to be really impressed with him.

Kal looked up at Rustam. "Okay, but are we going to get an advert?"

"Yeah, yeah, don't worry about that. If I get what I want then you get what you want." It was the kind of comment that was laced with real intent.

"Where you meet this one, Rustam?"

"Bahan ki friend hai... she's my sister's best friend."

"But won't your sister be pissed off? She must know you are dirty twat."

"Oh, forget about that. She is a grown woman, she knows what she is doing. I'm not doing anything wrong. Also, her dad is rich. They got proper money. Her name is Shazia, by the way, and she looks like one of the Spice Girls." He paused. "And she goes jogging and wears jeans."

You might well think what had the latter to do with anything, but Rustam was one of those guys who felt that if a woman wore jeans and exercised in public, she would be more likely to go out with someone like him.

We both sighed and I puffed out my cheeks. Something I used to do when I wanted to get out of a situation but then realised it was too late. This was not what we had signed up for.

"What the fuck has her jogging got to do with anything?" Kal asked.

Rustam leaned back in his chair again. "How many Asian women do you see jogging in Corpy Park?"

We both frowned and he was thankful the conversation ended there as Shazia walked into the coffee shop and spotted Rustam.

Rustam got up to greet her and sat back down and made the customary introductions. Shazia explained she was setting up a make-up and wedding company and we should feature her in the first edition.

"I want to create something unique for brides. Clients want something special for their big day and we can do this for them."

Rustam also liked the idea of using his religion as leverage. "Mashallah, it is good you are helping our community in this way."

Rustam was good at this and it was commonplace for some men to pretend to be religious so they could help to make the woman feel more comfortable. Rustam thought that Muslim women needed that 'safety barrier' when meeting other men and he was quick to use that to his advantage. It was a means to an end. I mean, who would not trust someone who is afraid of god, right?

She seemed to become more confident and went on to explain more about how experienced she was in her profession.

Rustam interjected again. "It is all halal make-up."

Kal had switched off a little by then.

"So how can we help?" I asked.

"How much is an advert?"

"It depends how big your advert needs to be?" I said, handing her our sheet with prices and sizes on.

"How about a full page?"

"That will be £300," said Kal. "But what are you going to advertise?"

"I don't know. I thought you guys would be able to help."

I had to be honest with her. "But you don't have a business yet?"

She hesitated. "I know, it has been not easy, but I want to put something in."

She began to get some money out of her purse.

Rustam looked across at us and winked.

"If I can pay you a deposit now of £50 and then I can pay the rest later."

She did not really know what advertising entailed and wanted to pay us money she clearly did not have. We had started out wanting to publish this newspaper by any means necessary, but then this just felt like a scam.

Rustam was looking pleased with himself. "She should be on the front page. You have so many great ideas."

Kal looked across and as had been the case since childhood he realised this wasn't the way things should be.

"How did you meet Rustam?" he asked.

"We met through his sister and he said I should speak to you."

It was time to just say we were fully booked for the month but then Kal always let down people with a lot more flamboyance than I ever did. I recollected once some years back we had a young man on Kal's course who was insistent that he would be the next Salman Khan. He had a stage name and was constantly making himself out to be someone he was not. I had always been polite enough to listen to his stories, despite knowing he was simply trying to convince himself. Once as he was in full flow amongst several people including some women he was trying to impress, Kal had just blurted out, "Thoree bullshit mariyah kar" (Stop this bullshitting). Ever since, I would sit there and listen patiently and wait for Kal to reach boiling point.

Kal glanced into his empty cup of tea. "The thing is at this stage we are just starting out. We can't do an article just yet. You seem like an intelligent person so maybe come back to us once you have set up the business in a few months. We don't want to take your money for now."

She looked surprised.

"But let me give you some simple advice. If you hang around with this pervert, you aren't going far."

There was complete silence. She looked across at Rustam and he back at Kal.

I smiled and then laughed.

Rustam wanted to say something but didn't have the nerve to do so.

"Okay, we are done here, Shazia, and if you need us in the future let us know."

Shazia got up, thanked Kal for being so honest, said her goodbyes and headed out towards the exit. Rustam remained seated and when she had gone turned to Kal and said, "What the hell, Kal?"

"What?" smiled Kal.

"You completely done me there. No way am I bringing any contacts to you again."

"Oh shut up, Rustam," responded Kal. "The only reason she is here is because you wanted to get off with her. We don't have time for this bullshit."

Rustam got up and slammed his hand on the table. "You two have got a lot to learn if you want to be successful in the media."

11 ZAIKA S. AKKAS

When nobody wants to be the boss then you must find one. There must always be an order in any organisation, otherwise it becomes increasingly difficult to get things done.

The evenings were becoming more and more predictable. We hit the streets during the day and met after 7 o'clock to discuss how we were going to publish a newspaper.

I had been to the town centre but not had the nerve to walk to into any businesses and spent the day window shopping and ended up calling Zak for a lift from a payphone. Only idiots called a mobile phone from a payphone as the conversation lasted seconds so the quicker you said what you wanted to say the better. Luckily, Zak had been driving close by and answered the call. It was probably the day I realised it was best I got myself a mobile phone, despite my earlier protestations.

On any given evening it could be at least three of us at the toilet paper factory. Today, we were all present for a change, trying to answer a perplexing question that needed to be settled once and for all.

"Who's going to be the boss?" Zak said, peering across from a pile of sheets. "We need someone to be in charge."

I had thought that was the job of the editor, but I don't think that is what he was referring to. I opted for the next best idea. "Imran is the eldest, he should be the boss and he also tells the best Punjabi jokes."

Imran stood up and then sat down. "I don't know."

That wasn't something that made sense to the others either. "We can't do that, that's just silly. This isn't mosque," said Zak.

"What are you saying, Zak, I can't be the boss?" joked Imran.

"No, you would make a great boss. Do you want the job?"

"Not really. Why can't we all be in charge?" responded Imran, wanting to be as diplomatic as ever.

It would not have gone unnoticed, but we needed to have someone to make the final decision as we were embarking on something that requires a multitude of possibilities.

Kal had an idea based on his 'research'. "No. We need something else. Something that makes us seem mysterious and rich. Our people love mystery and cash. A stupid guy with money gets more respect because secretly we aspire to the same false dream."

"Stupid cash guy," I said.

It would have been easy to be honest about things and tell people that we were launching the newspaper, but I don't think anyone wanted to take credit for the idea. We would rather not be the centre of the attention.

Firstly, nobody wanted to be the person who would have to tell the others they were wrong and secondly, none of us wanted to be the person who would take the blame if things didn't go to plan. The latter was my reason for everything really, I just did not want to take responsibility if everything began to go south.

It would also be far more exciting to have someone else responsible for fielding questions from members of the public anyway.

Zak was not convinced. "No, no, that doesn't work."

I did like Kal's idea though. A newspaper was not like any other product. It had to have a certain level of respectability to it and who would believe that a bunch of young men were able to take on that responsibility?

It needed a leader.

"What about a woman?" I said. "A woman owns Asian Image and she is this rich benefactor who has invested in this newspaper that is going to rule the world one day."

I wasn't entirely sure why this seemed like a good idea at the time, but it actually sounded better in my head. "And she has to be beautiful."

Zak, being self-professed 'male feminist' amongst us, wasn't too keen on my suggestion. "Why beautiful? What's that got to do with anything? No, she needs to be older, wiser and sophisticated."

"Why a woman?" asked Akeel.

I could sense Imran was a tad hesitant with what was in many ways quite a silly and childish idea.

Kal stood up from his chair, walked around to the tin of biscuits, opened it and took out four broken bits. It seemed he needed some snacks to prepare himself before unveiling his research. "Asian men bend over backwards for intelligent women. A guy walks in and we feel we have to outdo the son of a bitch." He took a few bites from his first two biscuits. "It is a completely different story when it comes to women, as we feel we have to impress her and even if she is out of our league we still think we got that one little chance where she might fall in love with us.

"Asian men can't say 'no' to women. No... let me rephrase that... men can't say no to women. Wait... Men can't say 'no' to nice looking, intelligent women."

Zak grimaced putting his hand over his face. "Wow, and you were going so well."

I agreed. In a roundabout way. "Heroes. We like to think we are some sort of saviours who will rescue her from her problems."

Kal was happy enough we had warmed to his idea. "Yeah... okay... and that. We need a name and it has to be someone believable."

For the first time in a long time the office was so quiet you could hear the fridge humming away in the corner.

"I got it," I said. "Why not use everyone's first letter of their full names. An acronym."

"Acronym," corrected Zak.

"Yeah that. Okay, ZAIKS. Come on, boys, come up with something."

Everyone began writing names on small pieces of paper and reading out a few names that came to mind.

"SAIKA?

"ISAKA?"

"Zakka"

"Ziki?"

"ZAIK. ZIAK AKKAZ?"

After what was only a few minutes and several mispronounced names later, Akeel stood up. "Here we go, lads, Zaika and Akkas. Zaika Akkas."

Zak, being ever pedantic for grammar and spelling, pointed out an anomaly. "We got two a's in the first name though and we need another 'S'?" But then admitted, "I guess it doesn't matter. Zaika Akkas."

Akeel was proud of his creation. "How about Zaika S. Akkas."

Of course you could say it like that, I put on a Punjabi accent: "Oh Zaika Akkaaas. She sounds real classy. The kind of woman you would take out just to watch her eat."

Kal seemed impressed but then asked the question we kind of wanted to avoid. "Zaika S. Akkas. What if someone wants to meet her?"

I knew we couldn't allow that. "No, she is far too important to meet anyone. She is our benefactor. You know like Keyser Söse, but she doesn't kill anyone."

Keyser Söse was the fictional character from the film 'The Usual Suspects' who stalks fear into a band of misfits.

"We don't actually know if Keyser Söse kills anyone?" said Imran.

What we liked to do more than anything else was make up background stories for fictional people. In this case, Zaika S. Akkas.

"Who is the main contact for her, then?" asked Akeel.

"I think it should be me." I looked over at the others. "After all, I am the one she trusts the most."

"Yeah, but now she thinks you are a little clingy," said Kal.

I wasn't amused. "She would never say that about me."

"Well, she did. She says that you used to be alright at the beginning but then as time went by you wanted more and more attention, but she is too polite to say anything to you."

This wasn't going the way I had planned. "Well, she says you are a complete twat."

Akeel and Imran laughed out loud.

Zak had already decided what this 'woman' may well be like. "She gets driven around and has a castle in Scotland. You can't get a meeting with her unless you are very important. In the meantime, we can pass the message on and she may choose to get back to you. We are her intermediaries. If she doesn't respond then she must be entertaining royalty in Monte Carlo on her yacht."

Wonderful, I thought. "Yeah, castles, Scotland, chauffeurs, Royalty, Monte Carlo, yachts and Blackburn. What's not to believe?"

12 CONTRARY TO POPULAR OPINION

Writing an article. It seems so simple when you see someone else do it.

Yes, we all knew how to put an essay together, but how can you sit there and write a story about someone and make it sound interesting? There must be some sort of trick to it. People are trained to do this, are they not? You can't just sit down and decide one day you want to be a writer. Or can you? And what about reporters? How do they do it?

I entered the office one evening, mimicking a cricket bowler with an imaginary ball. Sport had always played a huge part in our lives. Cricket and football were something we had loved from an early age. Some of us were better at it than others.

Zak and Kal laughed

"What the hell was that?" asked Akeel. "You do know you are 24."

"You never did that?"

"No."

"This kid in school did it all the time. We would run down the corridor and as we reached the end of the hall he would bowl."

The boy in question was addicted to this bowling action and soon enough it caught on. Anyone who ran anywhere would end the sprint by completing the bowling action. The weirder the action, the more laughs you got from your friends.

You then had to try to replicate the action of a famous cricketer. The one that got most people's attention was Abdul Qadir whose action, including the finger lick, could only be imitated expertly by one kid.

Kal remembered. "I know that. I did it too."

"And me," said Zak, and got up to show-off his bowling action. "Can't believe you never did it."

Kal then took a few short strides, swinging his arms wildly and following through by smashing his knuckles on the desk. "Ouch, shit."

Akeel seemed genuinely surprised. "Never did it and never heard of it."

There was more though,

"The best part is this," I said.

I took a short run up, completed the imaginary bowl and then held up my finger to mimic a leg before wicket (LBW) appeal, then wheeled away in celebration.

Akeel looked at me. "What the fuck is that?"

"It is called the full monty. Run up, bowl, appeal and celebration. You should try it. It is just so liberating."

"Excellent." Zak laughed. "Did you also not have a cock of the school?"

Akeel was puzzled. "Cock of what?"

Still warming down from my imaginary bowl, I said, "Cock of the school. You know the hardest lad in school. You know what I mean."

Akeel shook his head. "Never heard of that one before."

Zak stared at him with a blank look on his face. "You honestly surprise me sometimes."

"You were a nerd in school," said Kal looking towards me and then across to Zak.

He was right but being some sort of nerd was actually not that bad.

"Yeah I suppose I was." I paused. "You know what? I was more of a semi-nerd. I wasn't clever enough to be fully-fledged one. I was like one of those cool nerds who got on with people. You, on the other hand, were a nerd-basher."

Kal laughed out loud. "Hey, I defended a lot of nerds in my day."

"And beat the shit out of a few too," said Zak.

I stopped to drink some cola and then turned to Akeel. "What was your school like?"

Akeel had lived in Darwen, a town close by and it had been tough, with daily incidents of racism and bigotry. "It was so shit from day one," said Akeel, putting both his hands behind his head. "What do you expect? We arrived. We couldn't speak any English and they put us in a school of white people. What do you think was going to happen?"

It put our school days into perspective.

I shook my head and sat down to write, taking a large pad out of a folder on the desk. "Okay, I have been putting an article together."

Zak got up from his seat and looked a little confused after seeing me remove a pen from my pocket. "What are you doing?"

"I like to write it down before I type it."

"You can't do that for every story – it will take you months."

"Yes, but I like writing it down like this and copying it. I can't type straight on to the computer. That way I don't make any mistakes. Anyway, I don't know any other way. I like how this system works."

"You need to write it like you did at college. Remember that time when you wrote that essay. Do it like that."

"What essay was this?" asked Kal.

I had been in the same Economics A-level class with Zak. It was a subject neither of us was very good at. "I was writing an essay for Economics and we had this eccentric teacher who would ridicule all the work. Everyone was scared of him. Hated his lessons. Really made people feel embarrassed about their work by reading it out before handing it back.

"Then one day I came up with a new beginning to throw him and lo and behold he read it out in front of everyone in class stating it was some of the best work he had ever seen. You know that was the most satisfying moment of my life since I discovered the guitar solo in Bob Marley's Stir It Up at three minutes and twenty seconds.

"All that praise because I began the first sentence by stating 'Contrary to popular opinion…'. He said it completely and utterly engaged him and he just had to read the rest."

Those four words.

"Contrary to popular opinion…" said Kal.

"Contrary to popular opinion…" repeated Zak.

"Shut the fuck up," added Akeel.

I liked how it was possible to make even the most boring subject interesting. "Amazing. Just four words. Contrary to popular opinion, publishing newspapers is not as easy as it looks. Not any dickhead can do it."

Despite not looking forward to his class, we did have a newfound respect for him when during a session a bearded man with a mosque hat had opened the door and in broken English asked if he was in the right room. As soon as he had shut the door, several students had sniggered and laughed out loud, something our teacher had not been too happy with, telling us, "How good's your second language?" You could have heard a pin drop.

Kal was more practical in his outlook as always. "So, what's your point?"

"The point is, my educationally challenged friend, it is all about the first few lines. The rest can be total rubbish as long as the reader is hooked onto the first sentence or you come up with some amazingly catchy thing that rhymes."

I had done it. I had finally figured out what this journalism lark was all about. You didn't need any qualifications of any sort. You just needed to make boring stuff interesting by using complex words and phrases to bamboozle the reader.

"Yes." Zak nodded. "You also need the headline by the way."

"Yes, of course the headline is what makes the news story."

"And the story. It has to be a good story," said Kal.

"Yes, the story has to be good."

"And the picture," said Zak.

"Okay, the picture has to be special."

Akeel looked at me. "So, basically you know shit at this stage."

There was clearly a long way to go.

13 BOOK GIRL

Some people come into your life for a reason. Everyone else is just there to make up the numbers before you meet your maker.

Trying to get an advert was proving to be a problem for us. It wasn't easy convincing someone to part with their cash when you don't have anything to show them. We were selling blank space within a blank space.

With little success it was time to hit the road alone and try our luck with shops.

When you publish something insignificant there is always one thing people talk about. That one feature. That one article. That one part of your paper that unites everyone.

Behind the counter was a woman sat on one of those tall stools, reading a book. Her deep black hair tied up in a bun, she seemed to be watching the place for her dad.

"Do you work here?"

She put her book down and placed a marker at the page and peered through her thick glasses – the type of glasses my sister wore, like jam jar bottoms I would call them.

You could always tell a lot about anyone by the way they treat their book. Some are likely to place it face down on the table, others will turn the corner of the page over but only the conscientious reader has a marker. Well, it's my own belief that they generally must read a lot of books to invest in a bookmark.

"In a roundabout way," she replied in a what I could immediately tell was not a local accent.

I had been away for many years and met many people but the past two months I had gotten used to our familiar Lancashire accent or the 'hybrid talkers'. These were the people who were born and raised in the UK but still seemed to talk as if they had recently arrived here in the country.

"Well, either you do or you don't," I said, hoping to take back control of the conversation.

"I do." She definitely wasn't from this part of the country. My guess was she was had moved here from somewhere down south. Why this mattered at this stage and right now I don't know.

"Are you in charge?"

"If I wasn't so curious to know what you are selling I would be a little offended." It wasn't the response I was expecting.

I was still not convinced. "Well, are you?"

She sighed sarcastically. "Yes, I am in charge." She drew out the 'I'.

"So, why didn't you just say that?"

"I wanted to see if you were going to redeem yourself. Let's just say this is not going well for you."

It seemed unlikely I would be landing any sort of sale but decided to roll out the familiar pitch.

"Okay, what it is, we are launching a new newspaper for Lancashire and wanted to know if you wished to place a message in it."

"Like an advert?"

"Yes."

"Well, why didn't you just say that?" Touché, she had won our first exchange. "Do I not look like the store manager?"

"Well, if I am going to be honest, 'no'. I was going to ask you if you spoke English but obviously you do."

"You really know how to make a girl feel special, don't you."

"I didn't mean it like that."

"How did you mean it then?"

"What I meant was that you don't normally see someone like yourself sat managing a store. Normally it is some bloke who talks about cows and fields and wants me to tell him where I am from back home."

"Sorry to disappoint but hey here I am." There was that sarcasm again and it was already becoming quite addictive.

She paused. "We can talk about cows and fields if you want?"

It brought out a smile in us both.

Thankfully she turned her attention back to the paper. "What is going to be in it?"

"In what?"

"Your newspaper. What is going to be in your newspaper?"

"I don't know."

"Not much of a newspaper then, is it?

"Okay, what type of articles are you going to write."

"Things that interest people."

"What kind of things?"

I was taken aback by her attitude and lost for words at this stage. "You know, things."

I was going to have another try at selling her an advert. "So, about this message. We can offer you three adverts for the price of four as an opening offer."

"How wonderfully gracious of you?"

Thankfully, my poor attempts at sales were interrupted by a woman who walked in with her child.

"Hello Massi jee, what does little Adam want today?" All of a sudden I saw another side to her. She could be quite friendly and polite. Her mannerisms changed and I warmed to her a little.

I guess she wanted to come across as this cold individual but was using this as a way to deflect attention away from what was a genuinely kind and generous personality.

The child searched around the aisles looking for something like kids do and couldn't decide what to buy.

He finally picked up his sweets and accompanied his mother to pay for their goods.

As they left the store I glanced over at the book on the counter. It was a dark blue leather-bound copy of Pride and Prejudice.

"You like Jane Austen?"

Sales, I had noted, was all about trying to find something in common with your prospective client. That way you can talk about something you both like and the sale itself becomes something of an add-on.

In this case, I was genuinely interested in books.

At school whilst the other kids wanted to be prefects or take up some other insignificant position of power, I had been made librarian and spent a lunchtime and break times learning about the Dewey Decimal system. I hated how people would just dump their books anywhere. If I spotted anything in the wrong place in a public library, I would go place it on the correct shelf.

Putting books in order was a secret fascination of mine but never could I let on the fact that I liked the library and all the wonders it held. It was something you couldn't just shake off – not in my circle where men were supposed to be men.

Books, though, were my secret friend as they didn't judge you and didn't care what you looked like.

The woman seemed overtly interested in my question on her reading habits. "Her stories have got a certain etiquette and decorum that is lacking in the real world."

I rarely met any woman who talked books. I knew they were out there, but on the whole it was all about movies and the latest fads. I had got by on my jokes and impressions for most of my life, but I sensed this wasn't going to work this time around.

She was different.

"Have you read this one before?" I was not going to ruin the plot. There is nothing worse than telling someone the plot to a story especially when it comes to books, because it requires a lot of effort.

"Yes, but I like to re-read it as it is one of my favourites." Some people might think it is unusual to re-read a book, but we watch movies and classic TV moments over and over again, don't we? There is an enjoyment to be had on the pages of your favourite book that can't be replicated elsewhere.

"You know in the book the guy is only behaving like he is because he wants some attention and by being the opposite of what she expects in a man he draws more attention to himself. It is not a tactic I would ever use, but it worked for Mr Darcy."

I was quite proud of my take on a book I had not read. Having two sisters who loved watching period dramas had finally come in handy.

"Oh, that's an interesting way to look at things." She seemed to be impressed by my lazy analysis or was she just humouring me? I couldn't quite tell. "You read a lot?"

I wanted to tell her that I did in fact read some classics and would spend most of my nights tucked up in bed going through stories my older brothers had left on the shelf. Some of these I re-read as I got older as I did not understand them fully at the time.

But I think I will stick to telling her about the Doctor Who novels, which also took up a lot of my childhood. It is a lot safer for now.

"Yes, I do actually. Mostly, sci-fi books. I do like how you have managed to get hold of a classic Jane Austen book complete with a leather cover. May I?" gesturing towards the book.

She handed me the leather-bound book. "Isn't there something quite magnificent about a leather-bound book? The feel, the texture and the way it is put together."

"Are you going to smell it next?"

"Oh, not at all." How did she know that is exactly what I was going to do!

"So, back to your newspaper. What is it going to be about?"

"You know we don't know. We just decided to publish a newspaper and we are thinking about what it is going be in it? We thought it would be easy but now we need adverts to fund the first issue and things are not going too well."

She seemed to admire my honesty and made that face you make when you feel a little sorry for someone but don't want them to think you are pitying them in some way.

"Can I give you some advice?" Without waiting for a reply she added, "Why not have something of real interest in it?"

"Like what?"

"Like a page where people can talk about their problems without being judged."

"You mean like an agony aunt page?"

"Yes and no. You see, when anyone flicks through a newspaper, even the most stuck up reader will pause to look at the problem page. But with an Asian newspaper it must be different. Our people have a whole set of real issues they want to discuss, but they don't want to talk about them openly."

I had to admit it was a good idea.

"That's really interesting. You just come up with that?"

"If you didn't come through that door today then we wouldn't have had this conversation. So, well yes."

This had not been a complete waste of time at all. "What kind of problems do people have?"

"That's for them to tell you and then you need someone with a way with words to answer them in a fair and diplomatic manner. Someone people will trust."

She had a point.

"Yeah, that's really great; we will think about it."

I decided one last time to remind her about the advert.

"So, no advert then?"

She looked at me and for the first time in our exchange smiled. "You know sometimes it is better to quit whilst you're ahead. This was good."

I looked around the store. "So, you are always here?"

"For now, yes, but who knows where life takes us."

14 FRESHIE

Problems come in twos and so do solutions.

A newspaper has a duty to raise issues and create some debate whereas an Asian newspaper must talk about a set of issues because that is what justifies your existence. Anything else and people won't really take you seriously because you are printing information you are not qualified to talk about. So, it is best to stick to what you know.

Zak signed me up to Orange and ordered a Nokia 8810 which was nicknamed the 'Banana phone' because of its shape. It slid open to reveal the keyboard and I couldn't wait to show the others. "Check my phone out, lads. Chaudhry Shuiab Khan is now officially a tosser."

Kal had a Motorola and would flip open the end every so often, whilst Zak would constantly boast about his Nokia 6110's battery life.

I began to fiddle with the phone. "Are you on Orange, Kal?" Querying what network someone was connected to was one of the first questions anyone asked anyone when they first met.

I sat myself behind a desk. "Okay, lads, I am going to make my first sales call."

It was meant to be a historic moment but as I called the number

I hesitated and then asked for the owner of the business. The lady at the other end heard my name and promptly told me that he "didn't speak to Pakis".

"Man, I got racially abused on my first sales call, boys."

Kal walked across to my desk. "Give me the number. I will show you how it's done."

He typed in the numbers and when asked who was calling, he replied confidently, "It's Damian here."

The conversation was calm and measured and Kal took down the name of the owner. I gazed up at him. "That's some clever shit there, Kal."

"I used to do it all the time when I worked at the British Gas call centre. You should hear my Cecil. Nobody ever hangs up on him."

It was becoming increasingly difficult to stop people coming to the factory to see us. Later in the evening Rizzie entered the office.

Kal looked up. "Oh god, here we go." It was the kind of welcome Rizzie was used to.

Rizzie was Benny's twin brother and as talkative and opinionated as his sibling. Whilst one brother tended to be patriotic, Rizzie was the complete opposite and for that very reason tended to have more 'street cred'. I described him as a modern day Citizen Smith and whilst anyone else would be a little offended by the description, I think he revelled in it.

It was a mystery how these brothers had managed to get on and it helped never to have both men in the same room at the same time. To do so was like having an angel and the demon sat opposite one another at a dinner party – who was taking on what role on what day could well be a matter for a higher entity.

Rizzie sat himself down on a spare chair. "Relax, relax, I'm only here to see how things are going. Seeing as the boys are back in town." Little did he know these boys were not bringing much to the party.

"Things were fine up until 10 seconds ago," said Kal.

I put a cigarette to my mouth but didn't light it. "What do you want? We don't have any fags."

Zak was flicking through his Filofax again looking for a non-existent appointment. "Or any teabags. We have run out of tea bags. And sugar. And milk for that matter. Shuaiby, I told you to get milk."

"Sorry, I spent my last two quid on cigarettes."

Some said that Rizzie was a lot more intransigent than his brother and people would tell them apart by the fact that one had a moustache, and the other didn't.

Each would get stopped by people mistaking him for his twin. Once at a wedding, I recollect Rizzie being pinned against a wall by large burly man who said he was owed £10. I had to intervene and explain that this was in fact his twin brother and asked the man to look closely for any facial hair. It took some convincing but eventually after Rizzie showed him some ID the guy put him down.

Rizzie had his own ideas about this newspaper of ours. "I heard about your little project and I thought I would take a quick look at what you are doing."

Zak handed him a sheet of a page. "There. That is what we are doing."

Rizzie scanned through the page. "It is not going to be one of those arse-licking freshie newspapers, is it?"

If nothing else the brothers would introduce themselves to a conversation like the opening of a great musical stage play. It was right there in your face, full of colour, vibrance and stupendous sound, and was very hard not to be wowed by the spectacle. In Rizzie's case I had always warmed to the way he fought for the common man. The underdog. It was his thing.

"What is it with arse-licking with you two brothers? We just had your brother in here telling us how shit we are," I said.

"No, I think it is a good idea, but you have to speak out against the wealthy elite. Make them realise they can't take us for granted."

"Like mosque committees?" said Zak.

Rizzie shook his head. "No, the real power brokers who are helping to make us downtrodden masses work for peanuts whilst taking advantage of their privileged positions. As a newspaper you should be helping to bring these people to their knees."

"Mosque committees then," I said.

Kal seemed to encourage further discussion when there was no need. "How do you expect us to do that?"

Whilst he invited criticism, Rizzie did like to speak out against any injustices and he was not afraid to annoy people. It did not matter to him who was in the room or what 'status' this person had, if he felt there had been an injustice then he would call it out. It left some people angry and bemused. It takes a special kind of person to be able to irritate every single person in the room and then still be invited back the next day to repeat the whole process.

On this occasion he felt we should try to run before we could stand. "You begin by publishing a series of articles on how the British pillaged South Asia and how western powers are now creating puppet states across the middle east.

"Have you noticed how we always educate and entertain the families of despot foreign leaders here and then subtly help to keep them in power abroad?

"These states will also then be infiltrated by huge multi-national corporations which will then enslave these nations in a new kind of economic empire. When this is complete, they will ensure these nations are dependent on the goods and services they provide. Those nations will believe they are 'free' when in fact they are nothing more than proxy states there to buy our weapons and a McDonald's. It is happening right before our eyes."

Zak wasn't too interested. "We aren't that type of paper."

Rizzie seemed a little confused. "What type of paper are you then?" Again, he didn't wait for an answer. "Another rag whose job is to prop up the rich whilst the rest of us suffer at the hands of the fat cats. Corporate Britain and the Tory party should be on your radar from day one."

Rizzie was also the type of guy who you would love to be with if you ever found yourself at the bottom of a trench. He would find a way out and it was probably why I enjoyed it when he talked up things. "No way will WE ever let that happen. Not on my watch; I got your back, Rizzie." And I stood up to give a black power salute.

"Fuck the government and string up that bastard Blair. Just like Charles the first, 350 years ago! But first I have to write a piece on this cha cha (uncle) who says the council stopped emptying his bin because they are racist."

Rizzie laughed out loud. "Good man; it was 349 years by the way."

Kal wasn't impressed. "Oh, shut the fuck up, Rizzie. I don't see you suffering from anything. The likes of you benefit from the system. You are part of the problem. You talk all big about how the wealthy are grinding you down but secretly live your life on the back of all this so-called 'enslavement'."

It was all Rizzie needed. "You guys have a great opportunity to speak out and make them take notice or you can be the same as the rest – mouthpieces of the multi-millionaires who are taking us for a bunch of chumps. Or you could just write about a cat being stuck up a tree."

I was beginning to realise people expect you to behave a certain way and have a particular opinion when you work in the media. We were only days in and there were already expectations about what we should or should not do.

Zak sensed this. "We won't be mouthpieces of anyone. We are going to be completely neutral and print what is said, not what people want us to say."

Rizzie, much like his twin brother, didn't actually listen to answers. "Blah blah bullshit. All great ideas begin with a sense of honour and dignity, but you will soon change your tunes when you realise who the real powerbrokers are. The system is designed to keep us here at the bottom whilst rewarding the faceless elite. We have the highest levels of unemployment, poverty, and live in the worst areas. And they want to keep it that way."

I knew Zak was probably right, but I loved listening to Rizzie's rants. "I think I've heard enough, guys. Fuck the cha cha with the bin story. I suggest we bring down the council right now and declare a new republic right here in Blackburn. How we doing this, Rizzie?"

Rizzie laughed out loud and was buoyed by my new-found confidence in him.

He continued, "Don't be printing glowing stories about this piss-take of a country. It is shit. All we are good at is grieving over princesses and losing on penalties to the Germans."

Zak looked across at him again. "I like living here. Better than working in some field in Pakistan."

Rizzie sniggered. "You lot probably fuck that up too."

Kal again tried his best to raise the level of the discussion. "Why are we having this conversation with this guy? He is a prime example of the people who want all the benefits of living here but at the same time can't live without the system. It supports people like you."

Rizzie stood up and paced across the room. "I admit I am a product of Britain but some of us don't want to stay like that forever. I want to bring about positive change."

"But you are what you are? How can you not change?" asked Zak.

"I will tell you the truth and it is your job to act on it."

There was a reality that Rizzie was missing. "Like we told your brother. We haven't got a pot to piss in and you want us to change the world?" I said.

"Don't listen to him," added Kal. "This guy just likes to bark and wag his tail for biscuits."

Rizzie then moved on to one of his favourite gripes. "In years to come they will realise I was right about it all. Also, you need to sort out the mullahs."

"What's wrong with them? I know several Mullas and they are decent people," said Zak.

Rizzie sat back down and placed his feet on another chair. "Not those Mullas – Moulvis. They are dictating to us. This is Britain not the Islamic Republic of Blackburn."

"I knew it, it all boils down to mosque committees. Did we lose the mosque election again?" I said.

"Elections and you just don't go together, do they?" said Kal. "Anyway, why would we do that? What the moulvi's ever done? They do some great work. We are here to support the community in any way we can and tackle the huge levels of anti-Muslim prejudice."

Despite our banter and jesting Kal never let us forget that growing up, it was our mosque teacher who had a profound positive effect on his band of undisciplined pupils. In our case the small mosque based on Saunders Road had been led by someone we had always kept close to our hearts whatever the circumstances.

During our heated debate Imran entered the office and sat down across from Rizzie.

"Hey, look, another freshie is here," scoffed Rizzie before Imran had any chance to get acquainted to the conversation.

Nobody actually knows who uttered the term 'freshie' first. I guess it was used to describe someone who had recently come to Britain and was short for 'fresh off the boat'. What you will find with many terms used by British Asians is that they could be deemed openly racist if they were used by a white person.

Yet, here we were, using the term and over and over without a second thought about what it meant. In the seventies and eighties there was always a sense that we were in it together but in the nineties some of those born in Britain wanted to differentiate themselves from 'other Asians'. I never could see why, but I would think it made them feel more superior. We had more right to be here because we were born here, whilst the new arrivals did not.

The new arrivals were embarrassing us. I recollect sitting in a smoke-filled front room alongside many of the guests who would visit my father and one after the other they would share tales of how they managed to get through life on low wages, lack of language skills and the cold weather. A story told repeatedly was of one family friend who repeatedly found his toilet broken and could not figure how this was happening. He later learned a newly arrived cousin had been squatting and balancing on the toilet seat to relieve himself.

Once Rizzie heard this story he loved to repeat it and tease anyone he felt was a 'freshie'.

"What makes you so special?" asked Imran, who had come to the UK as a teenager.

"At least I ain't no freshie fuck."

"We are all freshies really at heart. Your dad was a freshie, was he not? All our parents were," Imran pointed out.

"Yes, he was at the time but now only people like you are real freshies."

I intervened. "Why people like him? Kal here was born in Pakistan so technically that makes him a freshie."

"Freshie is all about what you do, not where you are born. Take for instance Kal, like you rightly said. He is a freshie because he has habits like a freshie."

"Like what?" I asked.

"He just is. Like the way he talks and his mannerisms. His accent. He IS a freshie."

Imran didn't like getting into these 'philosophical' arguments with the brothers, but I could see this really annoyed him. Here he was having gone through life trying to fit in, but it had never been good enough for people like Rizzie. Then it probably occurred to him he was better off just being who you are and there was little point trying to please people who wished for him to have stayed in Pakistan. "None of this makes any sense. On the one side you say I am freshie because I came here when I was teenager, or on the other hand Kal is because he has 'habits' like a freshie."

Rizzie stuck to his guns. "That's my point: you are definitely a freshie."

Imran raised his voice. "I am bloody proud to be a freshie if being British is like you."

I applauded the comment. "The statement of the day award goes to… Imran the great."

Kal, who had also been denigrated during the discussion, leaned across the table. "What is your point? You seem to be skirting around the issue. Are you saying you are more intelligent than this guy because you were born here and don't like Pakistani things?"

The problem with Rizzie was that despite his grand calls for 'changes', which could well be genuine, once he got himself into an argument he found it difficult to admit defeat. "Yes, that is exactly what I mean. I am better than any freshie."

I had to point out another contradiction. "But you were calling for a mini revolution earlier. Why can't the freshies join us in the revolution?"

Rizzie seemed almost glad I had asked this. "Because they would fuck it up. They always fuck it up. Everything was fine before they started arriving here, making our lives more miserable than they already were. Freshies like him and his sort are what screwed it all up for the rest of us."

Zak had been listening intently. "Imran came to this country in his teens and is now educated to the same level as you? Would you agree?"

"I suppose so." Even Rizzie couldn't argue with that.

Imran looked across at everyone. "So, what does that say about you? You had a 13-year head start and we still ended up at the shit place."

We all paused and stared at Rizzie. It wasn't just Rizzie who had had a head start. We all had.

"Yes but…" said Rizzie.

"Hey, Rizzie, I love you but he's right." I nodded.

Kal stood up and tucked his shirt into his pants. "This guy has no point. One minute he wants us to unite and the next he wants to make out he is special and a little bit different."

Imran looked as us all again. "There are a few things that you need to know. I may be classed as a freshie in your eyes, but I am just the same."

"Why would you want to be the same as him? This guy is a knob," said Kal.

Imran wanted to point out something. "No we can't discount his theory just like that. He doesn't like freshies because they threaten him."

"Freshies don't threaten me."

"Yes, they do," added Imran. "You are afraid that when we peel away all the bits of Rizzie, at heart you will be treated like a freshie by this country. Like we are. Doesn't matter what job we get and where we end up and how rich you are, we will still be seen as immigrants."

It was something of an issue many of us had faced. No matter how hard some of us tried to fit in, to make ourselves better, we were still viewed as 'Pakis' by some folk.

Imran was keen to point this out. "You have this need to be accepted by this country so much and 'freshies' embarrass you. You would rather have it that we didn't exist so people like you could proclaim themselves to be 'true Brits'."

Rizzie had a way of wriggling out of any discussion. "I have no intention of celebrating my Britishness or helping Freshies."

Imran stood up and walked around to Zak's desk. "But you do. You must do both and it hurts you deep inside."

He was right, not just about Rizzie but all of us.

There was an awkward silence in the room before Kal stood up again to adjust his pants one more time. "Answer that, you freshie fuck!"

15 JOURNALISM FOR DUMMIES

After a while there was no home. You wake up and head out and then spend the rest of the evening in a backstreet factory trying to perfect something that you really have no idea about.

You can't jump into journalism, there has to be a certain level of training – or that is what you get told. You need to go gain a level of qualifications before you have the confidence to be put in front of a keyboard and type a set of words which will be read by a wider audience. Well, that is what normally happens.

Other times you must just learn things as you go along.

I was asked at one meeting whether I had any journalism qualifications and made to feel as if I was not best suited for this role. It was not the first time I had been told I was not good enough. At a school careers meeting the advisor had looked over my grades and thought it best I try not to go on to A-levels and maybe aim for something a little more suited to my 'academic achievements'.

"Benny was right, you know, lads," I said.

"About what?" asked Kal.

"About us not being proper journalists. I mean we aren't, are we, really?"

As Zak was the only one who had any semblance of media training, it was time to take a crash course in reporting.

I was surprised it had taken him two weeks and an inquisition by Benny to ask us what we actually knew about newspapers. "Okay, we need to learn some terms so we don't sound stupid in front of other people. I'm guessing none of you know shorthand?"

I was standing next to the fridge making myself a cup of tea. "I think you know the answer to that question."

Zak then gazed over at Kal who was scribbling down notes on a pad. "Kal, you need to design a masthead."

"A what?", Kal said.

"The masthead. The main logo thingy at the top."

Zak looked at us both and realised he may as well be speaking a foreign language. "A front page puff."

"A front page what?" I said, reaching for the milk.

"A puff?" said an already exacerbated Zak.

Kal shrugged his shoulders. "You are making all this up as we go along, aren't you?"

"That is the bit on the front page which helps to highlight a story inside. What about a by-line?"

I put my hand up. "Yes I know that. That is the name of the person who is writing the article."

"The page needs to be in columns."

Kal sounded a lot more confident. "Okay, makes sense. We will have six columns."

"Why?" asked Zak.

"Because we don't need seven. Six is fine." Kal laughed at having outwitted Zak who sighed again.

"Remember, we can't have any widows."

"Why not?" I said.

"Because they look ugly."

"He's right, we shouldn't have any widows." Kal laughed again, not knowing what a widow was.

A widow was a term used to describe a word sitting by itself at the top of a column.

"Okay, the folio goes here."

I walked over and perched myself at the end of a desk, sipping the tea I had just made. "The what?"

By this point Zak had realised that maybe he would have been better having this conversation a few weeks earlier. "In fact, leave this to me. Kal, can you put this together on Publisher?"

Kal stopped what he was doing and put both his hands behind his head and yawned. "Hey, I'm not completely stupid, you know."

Some secrets are made up to make ourselves feel more intelligent than we are.

It was also becoming increasingly clear that we didn't have an idea about what should be included in the newspaper. Everyone needs shortcuts, it is what gives us the edge. It was simple enough.

I sat down with my tea, and terms and phrases were all very well but what about the newspaper itself? "How do we know what is going where?"

Zak would help point us in the right direction again. "We have news here, here and here. A feature here. A picture story. Entertainment here and sport here."

I got up and walked over to his desk.

Kal joined me as we looked through his hand-drawn plan. It was scribbled together in a hurry with boxes drawn in different shapes on 12 sheets of paper.

"What goes here?" Kal pointed to a page with nothing on it.

Zak looked across. "We put some other shit on there."

It wasn't what I was expecting. "What do you mean 'shit' on there?"

Zak would love to talk up situations and ideas and by doing so he could quickly convince you that this was the way forward. In this case it was probably easier to tell us what might or might not be the best course of action because we were none the wiser. Today, his explanation sounded completely off the wall but still somehow made sense. "We can't fit everything in, so whatever is left and has to be included, will go on to the 'shit page'. Everyone does it. It is the boring shit that no-one is going to read but it has to go in because somebody paid for it."

Kal tried to rationalise the statement. "Like a business feature?"

"Yeah, you could call it that. But other shit too, like some council official we need to suck up to in the hope he may give us some adverts in the future."

I studied the blank sheet once more and sat down. "And newspapers do this?"

"Yes, all the time," explained Zak. "Whilst newspaper editors want to be seen as these great journalists fighting for the people – a lot of it is based on contacts and public relations exercises dressed up as stories. Posting the odd story to curry favours from people that might come in handy some time later. Or backroom deals made in posh bars or in our case the Hot'n'Tender takeaway."

Zak went back to flicking through his Filofax. "I may hate him, but Murdoch is the real kingmaker in this country. Why do you think Blair has been cosying up to him?"

Rupert Murdoch, the Prime Minister and international deals in high class restaurants were a far cry from the backstreets of Blackburn, but somehow it all made sense. "And there I was thinking it was all about ground-breaking stories and fighting for the common man. You just killed journalism for me and I haven't started yet."

Kal was still trying to rationalise the whole thing and was clearly intrigued as to how he may be able to use this peculiarly named page to his benefit. "The 'shit page' is the most important page in the paper then?"

"Well, 'yes' you could say that. It is still basically a page with the boring yet most significant shit on it. Thus, the name 'shit page'," Zak said confidently and closed his Filofax and slid it to his right like a man who had just completed a major board room meeting and now wanted his tea.

"I think I get it," I said. "What are we putting on there this month then?"

Zak sat back in his chair and put both his hands behind his head. "I don't know… some shit."

16 MIND YOUR LANGUAGE

What is written is more important than what is said. But what happens when you can't read what is written?

It was another bitterly cold day and Zak picked me up from outside my home even though I lived less than fifty yards away from him.

"Where we going?"

"Oh you will see." Which sounded a little ominous and he put on 'Heart' by the Pet Shop Boys. "I love this beginning."

"Just tell me. I hate surprises."

"Okay, this guy wants to meet us. He knows someone who is possessed with a jinn."

Really? Was this really where we were going? I took a cigarette out of my inside jacket and put it to my lips, opening the window at the same time. Realising how cold it was, I closed the window again.

"Honestly, Zak? We are going to see some exorcist guy? Bloody hell. Why didn't you take Kal or Imran to this one? I shouldn't be the bullshit Jinn guy." I looked up and puffed out my cheeks in frustration.

"No not the exorcist but the man who is possessed by the jinn. We will see the exorcist later."

I glanced across to him. "Did you ever think you would be saying those sentences to anyone ever?"

Zak decided to replay the beginning to the track again. "Let's listen to that first 30 seconds again."

His phone began to buzz and he took the call with his right hand. Thankfully, the family were unable to see us but would come to see us later. We headed to the office where Kal, Imran and Akeel were sat at three of the desks.

The office was already becoming far too small for our little operation and every night we would stuff more sheets into a metal cupboard in the corner. "Sooner or later we will have to build a website for this paper," said Kal.

I wasn't convinced it would be possible. "It is hard enough publishing this newspaper and you want to build a website?"

"I don't think so," said Zak. "I think there will always be a need for a newspaper because people like something physical to read. It is like books. There will always be books. People like to hold a newspaper in their hands."

"I don't know, Zak," interrupted Kal. "See how much money you would save by not printing. Something to think about."

"Nah, I can't see it," insisted Zak.

"I agree with Zak. This website stuff is just another fad," I said.

Imran had been busy going through some papers. "Are we doing an Urdu section or what, then?"

Any Asian media outlet had to be bi-lingual otherwise we would be missing out on a whole readership. Or so we thought.

The national Daily Jang newspaper was an Urdu newspaper which was read by people over a certain age. One of the things it did well or badly (depending upon how you saw it) was to have a mugshot of as many guests on a single page. It was one of the most complicated page designs anyone could ever see because each and every picture would have had to have been copied and pasted on to the page by a typesetter.

The reason this was done was because every single person could then be featured in the edition. It was a practice that was common in South Asia I got told. The more pictures you had in the paper, the more people would then buy it and then pass it on for others to read. It mattered little if the person was of any relevance, but if he had been in the crowd or on the front row he was in the paper.

Zak had a copy of the newspaper with him and threw it on a desk. "See this page here – you twats try to design this."

He pointed to a page that was a jumbled up mixture of headlines and pictures but somehow it worked.

"We can't do that, Zak." I picked the paper up and put it down in front of Imran. "That would take me months. There's about forty passport size pictures on that page. Anyway, who are most of these people anyway?"

"There needs to be some Urdu in the paper," said Imran. "What are you guys afraid of?"

Zak was sat at our one computer monitor. "We aren't afraid of anything. We just don't need it, that's all. Nobody reads Urdu." It was the kind of general comment that we had gotten used to.

Imran looked over at Kal. "Just because you guys don't read it doesn't mean other people don't."

Imran was right. There was a time not long ago when the translator was called into action. More often than not it was during doctor appointments. We all grew up in bi-lingual households and this need to speak to several languages was no more apparent than on a visit to the GP. When an elderly member of the family had to visit the doctor's, it was the translator's job to tell the doctor exactly what was wrong with their relative. That was easier said than done.

For some kids the pressure was a little too much. I recollect one friend telling me at school that he just had no idea how to explain that his dad had acid reflux or in his case 'gas'. We both laughed about it at the time, but years later I thought it must have been a tad humiliating for both the parent and the child.

Surprisingly, Kal wasn't convinced of the whole multi-language proposal. "The only problem I have is, if we put Urdu in then we have to put Bengali in and then a Gujerati page and then we have several pages of translations. Where do we stop? We just don't have the space."

Imran had not been one to shy away from raising questions that even we didn't want to answer. "Okay, let me ask you this. Are you embarrassed about native speakers as they don't fit into your idea of Britishness?"

"What's that got to do with anything?" said Zak.

Imran folded the Daily Jang paper and then unfolded it. "It is clear people like you don't think much of speakers of native languages as they are seen as a bit backward and only English speakers should be part of this paper. What can be more Asian than the language we speak? I thought we are trying to reach all sections of the community?"

Whilst we liked to think we were all inclusive even we had levels of prejudice which were difficult to hide. "This is isn't Mind Your Language, you know!" I exclaimed.

Mind Your Language was a late seventies TV show and one of the most cringeworthy national TV shows ever written. It was a show made by white people for white people, but we all watched it when we were kids.

"Hey, I liked Mind Your Language. It was funny, especially that Sikh guy," said Kal.

Imran frowned. "It wasn't funny, Kal. It was fucking offensive on a grand scale. White guy teaching a bunch of foreigners how to speak English. It was but but ting ting humour."

I laughed out loud, but he was right: Asians on British television were still either shopkeepers or single-minded parents who wanted to marry their daughters to the village idiot. If the writer really wanted to make us feel good about ourselves – a combination of both.

Zak looked at Akeel. "Come on, it was funny though. Bet you two could relate to it, couldn't you?"

Akeel laughed. "How the fuck could we relate to it – we speak better English than you guys do."

Zak chuckled to himself as he continued to type. "Yeah, but at the beginning you were like the Mind Your Language students."

Imran was clearly offended at this. "No we weren't. This is bullshit.

You see how this is panning out. You are the same as Rizzie deep down really, aren't you?" He paused. "The point is, people do read Urdu – and Gujerati for that matter – and they should have a dedicated page."

I shook my head again and was indeed concerned at anyone being compared to Rizzie the twin. "I am not trying to say everyone speaks English, but the majority of people do and those that don't can just look at the pictures."

Akeel shook his head back at me. "That's a bit offensive, even for you."

"You know what your problem is – that you can't speak Urdu," said Imran.

"Oh yes I can," I replied. "Aap ka Kya Haal hai maan." (How is your day, man.)

Akeel, Kal and Zak laughed out loud whilst Imran leaned back in his chair.

"See," said Imran. "Proves my point completely. You don't want to include it as you aren't able to fully understand it."

He was right but we didn't want to accept he had a point, and it was far easier if we didn't include any other languages.

"Okay okay, let's come to a compromise," said Kal. "We might be able to sell this translation service to some of the public organisations."

I glanced at Kal. "See, I was right, it's a scam thing, isn't it. We are only doing it so we can get white people to translate stuff for a minority of people. That way they think they are getting through to these people and then paying us for the service."

"Okay, why do they have Urdu signs up and leaflets in hospitals?"

"That's different," said Zak.

"How is that different?" added Akeel.

Zak stopped typing and turned his chair to face Akeel. "That is a certain sign and leaflet that might be able to assist an elderly person, someone who has just arrived in the country. We can have an Urdu page, but trust me in a few years we will drop it."

"Okay, let's just do what Kal said. Anybody wants it, we will translate it. Rest is English."

Imran grudgingly nodded his head. "We can go with that now as we don't have time to do anything else."

"And we don't do Bollywood," I said.

This was not the type of thing you were likely to hear from anyone looking to launch an Asian newspaper. Yes, Indian cinema was the staple diet of millions across the world and just as popular here in the UK and we liked Indian movies as much the next person, but the idea of having to base a publication around this was a little worrying.

Zak was not too keen on Bollywood and I was aware of some of the most famous films, but barring that we realised it wasn't our thing. "As much as I hate saying this next sentence, we are going to need to do Indian films."

Kal looked over. "Why, what's wrong with that?"

Imran was a movie fan and his knowledge of the film industry was impressive. "We can do classic movies."

"And jokes," I said excitedly, reminding Imran again, "you know, we could include the one about the blind fellow and his mates, these guys still haven't heard it."

Imran shrugged his shoulders. "I think if we can include that in a newspaper there may well be a riot."

Zak wasn't too happy with Indian films and I wasn't sure he had watched any. "We need to get away from this Bollywood really. Let's be honest, who really watches Bollywood? Hands up."

No one put their hand up. Imran then slowly raised his arm. "Does Maula Jatt count?"

Maula Jatt was a seventies Pakistani film where the main protagonist defended the honour of his village folk. It was a mix of 1970s low budget horror movie and a blaxploitation film of the same era.

"See, it doesn't make sense," said Zak. "It is a get-out clause for all Asian newspapers. You put a Bollywood story in because it is the only thing you can offer the readers. Everyone watches other stuff."

He had a point. "The last Indian movie I saw was Coolie."

Imran decided to go one step further. "Forced marriages, fundamentalism and stories about family culture should also be banned."

"We can't ban them completely, but it is a bit predictable all this," I said.

Zak was insistent that things needed to change. "I am not saying they aren't subjects we should cover, but there has to be something beyond Bollywood and arranged marriages."

"What about business?" asked Kal.

"We aren't really all interested in money, are we, or we wouldn't be here?" I said.

Here, was a time to change things. "Okay, whilst we will include

Bollywood, business and culture, they won't make up the vast majority of the content. We can leave that to the others and the nationals."

I wanted to add to that. "And no soppy stories about a guy who couldn't get married to the girl because she was a different caste."

Kal stood up to adjust his pants again. "Agreed."

"Fine," said Imran.

I gazed at everyone and raised my finger. "So, what does that leave us with?"

There was an embarrassing silence all around. Zak was about to say something but didn't. Imran looked a little confused as Kal turned his head away to some paperwork.

"Okay then, gentleman," I nodded and puffed out my cheeks. "Looks like we are going to have a few more of those 'shit' pages."

17 DO WE NOT DESERVE COKE?

When you lie about something it is better not to talk about it. It was easy making things up about yourself to sound more interesting, but problems arise when you try to keep up that pretence.

Kal and myself were en route to a community dinner event. "We have to be like 4000 Holes, the footy magazine?"

Kal was driving and had no idea what I had just said. "4000 what?"

"It's a small magazine," I explained. "Well, I wouldn't call it a magazine – it's a small pamphlet really that is sold outside Ewood Park." The term '4000 Holes', as many locals were well aware, was the town's claim to fame after being mentioned in the Beatles song 'A day in the Life'.

The first time my brother handed me this magazine I thought it was some sort of joke. We had collected match day programmes for many years, but this was different. It was like a guy had sat down in the corner of his bedroom and decided to write down his thoughts about football. And I loved it. But you had to be a football person to get the joke.

Kal was not a football person and never professed to be. "What's it like?"

"It's shit," I had to be honest. "In fact it is so shit it is good."

"And that is supposed to impress me?"

"No, I don't think you understand. It is full of these little things that only fans think about or would say out loud. There is no way you would find this in a normal mag as it is completely off the wall. The best thing is, it is probably put together by some poor bastard sat in his shed. We need to be like that guy."

It wasn't the future Kal had in mind.

"Not exactly like that guy, I mean. But you know what I mean. We need to print the type of stuff that only we get. The jokes we get. The shitty little stories that people hear when they are sat at the barbers. That way people will come back for more week in week out and talk about it at the next funeral. You know that kind of stuff."

We pulled into the car park of a community centre and Kal nodded his head politely. "Okay, but does it make any money."

"Of course it doesn't make any money. But that's the beauty of it."

"It is more a hobby then."

"Yeah, I suppose but you understand what I am saying?"

"Not really but as long as it makes sense to you that's all that matters."

Yes, it did make sense.

We made our way into the community centre and Raf walked past us, stopped and as was customary shook our hands. "How's it going laads?"

We had known Raf for many years and he had been away to university for a few months and returned with a cockney accent. I am not entirely sure why he did this, maybe it was his way of telling others he had been away. I had chosen to ignore the change in accent but of course Kal had not.

"Yeah, how's it going, guvnor?" replied Kal, mimicking what could best be described as a poor attempt at a cockney accent, which I probably think he did on purpose.

Raf raised his hand, laughed and walked away as if to suggest it wasn't the first time someone had brought this up in recent weeks.

"Why do you always do that, Kal?"

"What?" asked Kal, knowing full well what I meant by the question.

"Look, the guy wants to be pretend to be a cockney. Let him be. Why must you take the piss out of him."

"Because it's bullshit, that's why. He thinks he's better than us paindus (villagers) now? Once a paindu always a paindu."

There was always a hierarchy where we lived and for the most part no one minded. It was the way it was. We had the religious clerics, the community 'leaders' and the local politicians all vying for the attention of their own little clans and the white folk.

From the outside the stereotypical view was that we all followed these instructions and edicts were handed down from a higher power. Like sheep we all did what we were told. This made things simple for the authorities as it meant they had to only liaise with specific individuals and saved them the effort of having to do any real work. It also gave those 'gate keepers' a level of responsibility and a certain respectability to those around them.

Like I said, we really did not see this as any real issue. It was small clan-politicians making out they were more important than they were. Who honestly cared? I didn't and for the large part the others didn't see it as an issue.

Whatever the hierarchy was, we were at the bottom of the pile. We knew our place and it was better things stayed that way, for now.

The invention of Zaika Akkas had given us a new-found confidence. We were no longer a couple of young upstarts trying to launch a newspaper. We had a backer and she was important.

In truth, Zaika Akkas was a joke between a couple of guys who had been watching too many movies. You know the kind of thing that makes people think they are being funny and hopefully after a few months no-one will remember who she was. In a small town like this, any new person and her 'motives' can be amplified.

Both myself and Kal had both ended up at an iftari, an evening meal to break the fast (usually in the Islamic month of Ramadan). These type of events had more to do with the host using the occasion to either raise money for a suitable charity or to simply tell everyone what a nice chap he was.

Like most events of this nature, they tended to be all-male affairs and people were polite enough to listen to the speeches. I am going to be honest: we were both there for the food, like everyone else.

Anyone who has ever been to an Asian wedding and a gathering where food is being served to a large number of people will realise there is a level of chaos and order. It might all look like mayhem, but things are functioning efficiently – for the most part.

The tables were lined with plastic plates and it very much is a lottery if you get a seat at the first sitting. Thankfully, this being an iftari, there had to be one sitting. Any other day and there would be several layers of paper sheeting placed on each table. As one set of guests got up, the table would be cleared and another set of plastic plates, cups and spoons were hastily placed in rows. At very busy functions, people would stand behind you whilst you ate to ensure they got a seat at the next function. The pressure to eat fast and not linger was immense.

The hierarchy within our culture is on display at a dinner more than at any other time. We have those who are in the kitchen and must place the food into the trays and bowls. We have those who act as go-betweens and hand the food to the third set of people – the waiters. These waiters are the real workers and must then navigate the hall to ensure the meal is served appropriately. Of course, watching over this is the host himself who is joined by several other men of a certain status whose job it is to make sure everyone is carrying out the duty properly. The worst thing that could happen at this event or any other was for the 'rottee' to run out. This did not mean one was short of chapatis, but there was not enough of *anything*. So, most hosts would order extra food to make sure this shameful thing never happened to them.

People had their own habits at these dinners too.

Kal preferred to fill his plate with chutney (mint sauce) before any of the main food had arrived, as he felt it gave him a head start on everyone else. Another man to my left placed salad on his plate and pick at it like a rabbit. Every so often someone would walk past and shake hands with everyone. And I mean everyone. Not just the person one recognised but also the fellows sat to his right, left or in front of him.

"Okay I have to go take a piss," said Kal and promptly got up.

"May as well do the same." I was not sure why I said this as nobody was listening. I walked a few paces then returned and took off my jacket, leaving it spread over two seats.

Nobody likes to use urinals if it can be helped. There is nothing more embarrassing than queuing at half time at a match at Ewood Park. I once waited for five minutes and when I got to the front I just couldn't go. The bloke behind me was only a foot away but the pressure was too much and the floor was normally full of urine by the time it was your turn anyway.

It was busy as people liked to wash up a little before food was served. We waited for one of the cubicles to free up.

A man had walked in ahead of us and proceeded to urinate in the cubicle and then flushed the toilet before he had finished. He finished off and made his way out of the cubicle.

"You need to flush at the end, brother," said a disgusted Kal.

"What?" The man looked a little shocked and embarrassed at the same time.

"You need to flush the toilet again."

"I did flush."

"Yes, you flushed but you need to flush again. I noticed you flushed whilst you were clearly in mid-flow. You have to flush again otherwise the next user will be left with the impression you have not flushed at all."

He returned to the cubicle and studied the bowl and then flushed the toilet again, smiled and then walked out without washing his hands.

"See," I said, "I hate it when they do that. I bet he's going to shake some poor bastard's hand now."

"As long as it isn't mine, what do I give a shit."

Kal entered the cubicle, locking the door behind him and flushed again for good measure.

We returned to our seats to find Mr Younis sat in front of us.

Mr Younis was a local businessman and someone who liked to think he had some sort of power.

"Aay," shouted Mr Younis over to the waiter. "Come here."

A nervous young man hurried over to our part of the long table. "Yes, uncle?"

"Forget yes uncle, you have served the ghosht (lamb curry) but what am I going to eat it with? Fresh air?"

Mr Younis looked like a sober version of Father Jack of Father Ted fame. I almost expected him to shout out 'Feck! Drink! Girls!' whenever I met him.

More than anything else he was the type of man who liked to demean others at weddings and social functions. I think he revelled in it as it allowed him to do two things. Firstly, he could shout orders at people who had no other choice but to accept them, and secondly, he could 'impress' others in the vicinity who may not know who he was.

The young man nodded his head.

Mr Younis took hold of his hand. "And look across the table, what do you see?"

The waiter who was actually not a waiter and had probably been coaxed into serving the food at the last minute had a confused look on his face.

"I will tell you," continued Mr Younis. "I see coke bottles on that side of the table and only 7up on this side. What? Do we not deserve Coke?"

The man stood there motionless as if some great crime had been committed.

"Well, do we not deserve Coke?" repeated Mr Younis, this time with the air of real authority, like a headmaster.

"Yes, you do," he replied nervously.

"Then go fetch me some and make sure it is a new bottle."

The teenager hurried away to find some Coca Cola bottles and returned in seconds with two bottles, placing them both in front of Mr Younis who was still not impressed.

"You know, our young generation have no idea how to serve rotee anymore. Hope he doesn't bring us them second-hand bottles."

In this case 'Second-hand bottles' were those that were made up of the contents of other bottles. To ensure no drink went to waste in the back and away from the prying eyes of the guests, one young man would sit in the corner with a funnel. His one job was to fill cola bottles out of the half empty ones.

I don't think Mr Younis had anything to worry about today as there would only be one sitting.

Mr Younis turned to the man next to him. "Lucky we aren't at an

Indian dinner. They gave me one chicken piece last time."

There was also a distinct difference between Indian and Pakistani weddings. Pakistanis loved to show off how many servings they could handle. Indian events tended to be more low-key with some having the 'one chicken piece rule' to which Mr Younis had been referring to. That is not to say one spent less than the other, but an Indian function tended to focus on endless amounts of biryani.

We both sat there hoping to hell he was not about to turn his attention to us. Unfortunately, we were next on his radar but thankfully he seemed to have something else on his mind.

"That film Titanic is coming out?" said Mr Younis looking towards me. "What's it about?"

I glanced up at him. "It is about that ship, the Titanic."

"What happens?"

I smiled and then looked over to Kal who was busy filling his plate with some salad now. "Kal, do you want to tell Mr Younis what happens in Titanic."

Kal kept peering along the table towards the kitchen area. "It sinks in the end."

"Oh, that isn't nice at all. Bit depressing then. They could have made a better ending than that."

Mr Younis didn't seem concerned at all that he knew nothing of Maritime's most infamous disaster of the twentieth century.

I began to correct him. "I don't think they could do that. It is a true story. You know… forget it. Doesn't matter."

Kal's phone rang. "Hello… Hello… HELLLLO." He flipped the

phone shut. "Crap reception here."

The remainder of the food began to arrive and was placed in front of Mr Younis who had purposely cleared the area in front of him for the waiter. If nothing else, he knew how to get fed first. "It all boils down to drinking and women."

"What?" asked Kal.

"These are two things that are completely at odds with British and European culture. We can dress it all up in these different ways and talk about these conspiracy theories all day long, but it has to do with women and drinking."

In between mouthfuls of food I said, "What do you mean by that?"

"In our culture drinking is frowned upon. I am not saying we don't do it, but the whole British culture is based around drink. When I worked in a factory we would get along all day long but at the end of the night they would go for a drink and I would go home. And women. We like to keep our women shielded and they tell their women to behave like men."

I didn't even know how to respond to that. Thankfully and not for the first time Kal said what was on my mind. "That is so wrong, uncle. Where did you hear that? You have a very narrow view of all women and British people."

"It is true though, isn't it. Drink and women. Take those two things out of the equation and we are the same."

Mr Younis then got up from his seat to welcome another councillor we had spoken to in the past. He sat down next to Mr Younis and began to pour some curry into a plastic bowl.

The councillor looked over to us. "So then you two. I hear you are publishing a newspaper? Who is the person in charge of the paper?"

"It is us," I said.

"You guys? No, I meant who is funding you?"

"We are," said Kal.

"So, you have nobody funding you?"

Mr Younis looked at us both as he began to fill his plate up with more lamb curry.

I nudged Kal. "I think he wants to know who is REALLY in charge."

"Oh, you mean who is our benefactor. Well, that would be Ms Zaika S. Akkas," added Kal.

Mr Younis seemed interested in us again and loved to hijack conversations. "Ms? Do I know her? What does she do?"

We had of course prepared a background story of sorts. "She runs some successful businesses here and there, and wishes to venture into the media industry," I said. "She is Scottish, you know and lives in Aberdeen."

For some reason I said 'Aberdeen' in a Scottish accent. The origin story would help to ensure that no one would do any background checks, or so I thought.

Mr Younis frowned, paused and then his face lit up. "Oh you mean Zaika Bajee. Yes, yes, yes I know Zaika Bajee. Oh, I know her well."

I turned to Kal and he back at me. Was there really another Zaika Akkas? Or did he know we were lying? "How do you know of Ms Akkas?"

"Well, she is someone I used to work with in my younger days, you know. Very nice lady. I also know her husband; I visited them both in Aberdeen."

Wow, she had a husband and she really did live in Aberdeen. Shit.

"Are we talking about the same Zaika Akkas here?"

Mr Younis continued, "Yes, yes. Oh councillor saab (sir) they are friends with Zaika Bajee. Wonderful lady. Wonderful idea of yours too. Maybe would be good if we arranged a meeting sometime and I can tell you more about what I am doing for business people here in the community."

The councillor nodded his head in agreement.

I wasn't entirely sure if he had worked out we were a bunch of charlatans or there was someone else named Zaika Akkas. Surely not?

Kal laughed mischievously realising who the real charlatan was. "You know, the next we speak to her we will give her your salaam. As you know she is a very busy lady."

Mr Younis nodded and wiped away the curry from his mouth. I know it was a small thing to notice, but he was an efficient eater and would pick through the bowl to ensure he got hold of the best pieces of meat before anyone else. It was a skill few people had. And then having picked at the meat he would then place the bones in the middle of the table. Not a single morsel of food ever went to waste, and if he spotted someone had not cleaned their plate, he would make a point of telling them.

"Yes, Yes, definitely," insisted Mr Younis and pointed at the chapati on my plate. "Are you having this?"

"No, help yourself."

Mr Younis polished off the remainder of the curry on his plate. "That was nice, I wonder what's for dessert?"

18 CHEQUE PLEASE

There had been a battle going on ever since I was young. There were those who said we were far too religious and there were those who said we weren't religious enough. Finding a balance was never going to be easy.

What you might think was acceptable for one person was deemed outright offensive to another. Reputations could be won and lost in an instant. One time at a Young Muslim conference I had attended, an eloquent speaker had been challenged over a remark he had made about the Iraq War. The speaker had stupidly insisted that at times it was 'permissible to ask for the hand of the devil if you find yourself drowning'. He was called out publicly by several audience members who were quick to denounce his words, which at the time I did not fully understand. He was never seen in the same light again.

Something struck me very early on. There was never a question of 'bad Muslims' and 'good Muslims'. This was nonsense. It made it easy for everyone else who couldn't actually be bothered exploring the real issues in our community. Sadly, sometimes we would do this to ourselves. Whenever we had met anyone with any knowledge of the religion, they had almost always turned out to be genuine folk just trying their best to get along with a humbling quality about them.

It was a late Thursday afternoon when myself and Akeel had been invited to a small travel agency where we were greeted by a man with a large beard and jubbah (a long Arab-style dress which was becoming more and more popular with some Muslims).

He had heard about what we were doing and asked to meet us at this office. This, at the time, was quite unusual because until then we had been cold calling small shops. To be invited to an office personally was a major bonus at the time and a huge confidence boost.

The travel agency looked as if it needed a bit of a makeover, yet the owner was immaculately groomed. The office area also smelt heavily of Arabian scent perfume which wafted immediately around the room – and, we later learned, latched onto our own clothes.

"Aslamuliakum, brothers." The manager shook us both by the hands.

"Walalamuliakum," replied Akeel and then looked at me.

"Aslamuliakum, sir. I rang earlier about our newspaper."

Now, normally there would be a level of pleasantries where we would get the chance to explain the background to the edition and any hopes and dreams we had for our fledgling publication.

But we were quickly learning things don't normally pan out the way you initially thought.

"Yes, a newspaper. It is for Muslims?" This it turned out was not the first time we had been asked this question on our short travels. It was becoming a little tedious to be honest. I could sense Akeel hated this question but was polite enough in his response. "No, it is for everyone."

"Everyone? Why not just Muslims?"

This time I replied, "Because people of other religions are living here too."

"Like who?"

Maybe he would be a little more accommodating if I told him who we were talking about. "Hindus, Sikhs and even some Pakistani Christians."

Without letting me finish he said, "Forget them kaffirs."

Now, at this point, normally anyone trying to sell something would quickly realise that this is not exactly going to plan and maybe head for the door. But we couldn't do that. We knew now we were about to be sucked into a conversation that neither of us really wanted to get involved in.

In Akeel's case this was going to be more frustrating than for me. Having grown up as someone who had learnt the Quran by heart and acquired a great deal of knowledge along the way, he rarely if ever wanted to correct others when challenged in this way. It was a level of humility I saw in few people if I am going to be honest.

In this case we had been invited to someone's office who then wanted to tell us how to run the newspaper. And here came the follow up question that looked to put the onus back on us. "They get their own paper. This should be for Muslims. Aren't you both Muslim?"

"Yes we are." Great. Akeel would talk to this guy.

"Then do a newspaper for Muslims only."

"It is an Asian newspaper for Asians… and anyone else really," responded Akeel.

This, I could sense, was about to descend into one of those conversations more about us and who we were. There are many things we take personally and one of those is anyone who tells us what to read. I cannot envisage a person being invited into an office and trying to sell an advert and being asked the next question.

"Will you have pictures in the paper?"

It was the kind of question which we both knew would eventually lead to something else. The idea was to tempt us into a religious debate and discussion and one which we both knew we were unlikely to win. Not because of a lack of knowledge, but it was increasingly common to get into these debates about minor religious gripes with people. I would get frustrated with these discussions as I knew no matter what I said, it actually made no difference to the other person and soon it became a matter of a small war of attrition with one side not willing to back down in case it dented one's pride. It was very much like trying to pitch a tent in high wind. You know you have to do it, but sometimes you just can't be bothered and would rather spend the night blown around in the cold.

Akeel, meanwhile, had picked up on this and decided it would be best at this stage to play along. "Yes. We will have pictures in there, black and white at the moment but as soon enough they will be colour."

There was another pause before the man told us, "You know taking pictures is haram."

Oh dear. We were in the halal-haram zone now. This is a zone where only the most ardent debaters should venture, and we were not one of those. These short sharp statements would cut through most people. I had had enough. "I see. This is going nowhere."

But we were not done yet and what followed was an exchange between the office manager and Akeel.

"What about women?" asked the man.

"What about them?"

"Will there be any women in the paper?"

"Would you like there to be women in the paper?"

"Yes, but only if they are fully covered. Unless they are non-Muslim women – then you can show their face."

"I am not sure we could do that."

"Why? I thought you said you were a Muslim?"

Akeel sighed. "Okay, what about the advert you wanted to place."

"Yes, we have plenty of money for that."

Oh good, we were finally getting somewhere.

"But, if you let me have one free advert and then I can see how it goes and place the next one."

I couldn't take this anymore and muttered an expletive under my breath.

Another awkward pause followed before the man decided to take things to another level. "Do you know the media is controlled by the Yahoodis (Jews)?"

"I think it is 'cheque please' time now, Shuiab." It was fitting that Akeel should use this term at this time.

'Cheque Please' was the term used by the character played by

Sanjeev Bhaskar in the newly aired Goodness Gracious Me. In the sketch everything is going well for the man on a date before he decides to utter an embarrassing comment and as his date leaves he follows that up with the hilarious words, 'cheque please'. This was worse than a bad date.

We both decided to get up from our seats and I sighed. We had not been summoned here for a meeting or for any business opportunity. We had been called here so this man could tell us what bad Muslims we were. He had no intention of placing an advert or wanting to support the newspaper in any way. He had simply wanted to act more superior and have us sat at the other end of his desk so he could tell us exactly how things should be. And as was normally the case when one is embroiled in discussions of this nature, it was time for our host to play the guilt card.

"Brothers, do you know every single sin in the newspaper will be on your heads on the day of judgement?"

You see, this is where things would get a little too personal. The strange thing is this – it was very easy to heap a whole load of guilt on other people by linking certain acts you were doing with religious texts and sayings. If you could make the links, however dubious, you could in fact encourage the other person to come over to your way of thinking.

It was a great way of deflecting the attention from the discussion that needed to be had to something that put the blame of society's ills back on to you. How on earth did we end up here? We only came in to get an advert.

I decided it was best we left on amicable terms. "Thank you, this was really, really interesting. You have been a great help."

Akeel though, I noted, would always subtly have the last laugh.

"You will thank me one day…" said the man.

"I can tell you now whatever happens… we won't."

With that we left the office feeling a little dejected.

Later that same day we headed back to our own base. It had been a long afternoon visiting businesses and the evening was our time to produce the goods, but we had little to show for the day's efforts, again.

Sat there as always were both Zak and Kal. Zak was busy on the computer.

I felt we needed to find a new direction.

I walked over and sat down on the leather chair. "Okay, lads, this is not going to be easy. This whole thing is one big joke. Let's just quit now whilst we can."

Zak and Kal stopped working and looked over at us. "Why, what happened?" said Kal.

Akeel stood in the corner with his arms folded. "We met a dickhead, that's what happened. Some of these bloody Moulvis (preacher/imam) will bury the lot of us one day."

"Woah woah, Aki you can't say that… okay," I paused and sat up. "Yeah okay then but he wasn't no Moulvi." I slumped back into my chair again, exasperated.

Kal sighed and smiled. "You know what your problem is. You are anti-Muslim."

I glared at Kal and then at Akeel. "Don't be pulling that bullshit on me. Today is not the day."

We had the familiar debates with a lot of people through our teen years, including with those who were deemed to be 'extreme' in their interpretation of Islam. To me though they were just people. Kal and I had made good friends with some of these young men and I genuinely felt they were decent folk trying to make their way through life, but it just wasn't appealing to us at the time. After the first few months some of the more persistent ones left us alone, which at the time I felt a little let down by – "It was like talking to one of those HT boys but without the cigarettes, Kal."

I guess it was my frustration bubbling to the surface once more, but I eventually got the laugh I wanted.

Kal laughed out loud. "Oh yes, I remember those days."

"You know what the strange thing about some of those guys was," I explained. "Everyone had a moment of deliverance. You know they all had a back story about being a gangster and then they saw the light. It was bit of a cop out, though, wasn't it?"

For some of these members we noted much of this back story tended to be exaggerated to fit into a particular narrative. "You know what?" I added. "It would be good to meet someone who doesn't reveal what a son of a bitch he was and now wants to tell me to be a better person. Here's something… don't be a twat in the first place."

Akeel sat down at a desk and put his feet on the table. "Like Kal."

Kal looked a bit confused. "What do you mean… like me?"

I laughed. "He's right, Kal you were a bit of a twat. Not to us but to everyone else. Most people who meet you for the first time think you are a grade 'A' twat. How come you never went through the 'phase'? How come you haven't gone through this wonderful transformation?"

Akeel chuckled to himself. "Maybe he is still a twat, that's why."

"Can you stop calling me a twat," said Kal. "I was just finding my way like everyone else. Anyway, some of those guys were only doing it for the women."

Kal had raised this very point in a discussion before and had insisted some wanted to play the religious card to find a suitable match, and once that was in place, they soon lost interest in the 'cause'.

"That's a story," interjected Zak, "that would make a really good feature."

"Oh, and the girls did it too." Kal was as always being dangerously honest in his analysis. "One minute they wanted to hang out and next we would see them with a headscarf on saying 'Mashallah', calling me 'brother'. The lengths people will go to find a halal boyfriend the haram way."

I chuckled to myself. "So then, when you doing it then?"

"Doing what?" asked Kal.

"Wearing a headscarf."

Akeel laughed out loud. "Yeah a total transformation to make up for all the people you pissed off over the years."

19 IT'S A SCAM ISN'T IT?

If there was one thing that we hadn't discussed at length it was the reason for our existence. We were trying to publish a newspaper for 'Asians' and the comments by Benny earlier had been playing on my mind especially since my attempt to change my name to 'Paul'.

It was not easy keeping oneself motivated. This was not the first time anyone had published an Asian newspaper and Asian radio stations had been firmly established for a while. But these seemed to be completely at odds with what we had actually wanted.

People like to think there is a shared idea about how we should be perceived, but there isn't. We were not one unified set of people and banding everybody under the 'Asian' banner didn't make any sense to me. There are a whole myriad of ideas and people.

Another evening in the factory; it had been a counter-productive few days and conversation drifted towards this word 'Asian'.

It all started off well.

"Being Asian is cool at the moment," exclaimed Zak. "Everybody wants a piece of the action."

Zak has always remained upbeat, probably because he had been at this conjuncture before. "You have to get the first edition out and then things will fall into place."

Kal agreed. "The first edition is what matters. Let's see how it goes from there."

If there was one thing about Akeel it was his ability to be totally upfront. "Maybe we are not cut out for this stuff. It is just a big scam this really, isn't it?"

A scam? That was a different way of thinking about. Maybe scam was a harsh word to describe it.

Zak was curious to see where Akeel was going with this. "What do you mean?"

I was back pacing the office with an unlit cigarette in my hand and pretending to behave like some sort of philosopher. "I think I know what Aki is saying."

"The whole thing. Being Asian and Muslim and wanting to be part of something. People just want to scam the system. Think about it – there really is no need for any of this. Maybe Benny was right: what do we need an Asian newspaper for? Why do we need an Asian anything?"

There was awkward silence in the room as everyone digested what I had just said.

Zak flicked his pen, checked his phone again and placed it back into his pocket. "In an ideal world I admit there is no need for 'Asian' anything, is there. Why do we need it? But we aren't living in an ideal world, are we?"

Kal walked over and took my unlit cigarette off me and removed his lighter from his trouser pocket before remembering he was standing in a paper factory. "There is nothing wrong with the idea of an Asian paper." Kal always did see things in simple terms. "There is a market for an Asian newspaper that people want to read and we are filling that niche. It is not that difficult."

Zak took out his phone one more time and skipped through some numbers which made a beeping sound. "If the mainstream newspapers were doing their job properly then there would be no reason for us to be around at all. I'm not asking for any special favours of any sort. The only time they print anything about us is to perpetuate that stereotypical view of what we are like."

I scratched my chin. "Are you also saying white folk can't write about Asians? I'm sure they can?"

It seemed Zak had been asked these questions before. "No, I didn't say that. I just think when they put something together, they may not have knowledge we might have. They may skirt around an issue or just write things from a white person's viewpoint. It comes across really patronising. They just don't get it.

"And a lot of the time they throw pennies at us to make out they are doing us a favour."

It was a theme Zak would regularly bring up in our discussions that to be accepted we should never just settle for second best. A lot of the time senior executives want to shut down ethnic minority talent by offering them sub-standard roles or the odd contract. That way they could not be seen to be ignoring Asians and other ethnic minorities, and those 'pennies' were a lot more use to them than they were to us.

"Also, you have a load of go-betweens like that dickhead you guys met who take the crumbs and massage their own egos at the same time."

Maybe it was time to raise some more home truths. "I guess so but a lot of the time it is nonsense, isn't it. A lot of the time we have people just using their race and culture to get preferential treatment. We know full well it is bullshit, but they still manage it."

I was starting to sound like Benny, but it was probably due to the fact that things were not going as well as I thought they would. This was meant to be fun and we were meant to be this successful bunch of young entrepreneurs, but it had not turned out that way.

Kal was not about to let me put a complete downer on things just yet. "I don't think that is true at all. If you can't provide a service, then someone else has to step in, don't they? That's how all this works, isn't it?"

I wasn't finished just yet. "I'm just saying we got people in positions for the sake of it. Everyone has a bullshit story to 'stand out from the crowd'. Normally, it is the same old tale just told in different ways. My backward culture kept me down and one day I realised I can be anything as long as I aspire to follow the British way of life. We got sold the Disney story and we are acting it out because that is what sells. It is all bollocks. We all know people only do it to make themselves a quick few quid."

"There is that," added Zak.

"Then you have the folk who want you to believe they are selling shit in the halal way but in reality just want to milk you dry without feeling guilty about it. You know, if me and Aki had just agreed with that guy we would have got the advert. He would go home safe in the knowledge he had helped the 'Muslim Ummah' and I would bank the cheque." I was getting pretty frustrated with the whole thing and it showed.

There was silence in the room again and this one lasted a lot longer than the others.

Kal, though, was adamant as always. Maybe he knew something I didn't. "Your thinking is all wrong. The reason we are where we are is because we refuse to go down that same path and there will be others like us."

Having lost the argument I tried to pull out my other trump card, that of abject failure. "Look at our predicament – it has little to do with our culture; it has to do with the fact we are shit at stuff."

"We aren't," said Zak.

"I am," admitted an all too honest Akeel.

Kal was tiring of my depressive take on things. "You really know how to see the negative on things. The reason we are doing this is to see if we can beat the system with nothing."

That was the only thing that was keeping me from going crazy at the moment.

Akeel was always good at putting things into perspective. "For the first time in your life you have nothing at all to lose. If it works – it works. If it doesn't, we go back to being the pricks we are."

The thing about trying to create anything new with friends is that you can always rely on conversations like this to end on a more positive note. If this had been some sort of business meeting with work colleagues, no one would have been able to speak their minds. We would have had endless discussions and strategy sessions about what to do next and if our work structure could be improved.

There was no time for this in the real world when you have nothing but your wits and personality to get you by.

It was better being brutally honest about our predicament, something Kal had always been throughout his life. "That's the best advice anyone can give you. We do it and see what happens. If it doesn't succeed and we aren't here in six months, we let some other knobs try it. But until then I suggest we get back on the road tomorrow."

Zak was a little more to the point. "Nobody is going to try it. Not here anyway. It's far too much hard work."

He was right. "That we have, Mr Khan," said Kal.

There was yet another pause as we tried to contemplate if we were in fact wasting our time and setting ourselves up for one big failure.

Of course, I had more to say as always. "I just think some people are just good at the manual stuff. I am good at the manual stuff. This having to sell and write is not for me."

It seems, however, that Kal had had enough. "Have you had your rant? Can we get some work done now?"

I walked over to his desk and retrieved the cigarette he had taken from me earlier. "Yeah. I'm done."

20 INDIAN-PAKISTANI

If you are ever invited to an Asian household then there are a couple of things you should know. First of all, you should never eat too little because the host may think you don't like their food. Secondly, if you are woman then you are not going to get served until the men have eaten. And finally, prepare yourself to be ridiculed if you can't speak your native language properly.

"There is a battle going on and you guys are going to be on the losing side." Uncle Hakim had a habit of raising issues when there were none.

There is a distinct difference between how cultures respond to death. Within western society death is seen as something quite private and there is a tendency to leave the bereaved alone. After the initial messages of support there is this feeling that the family or friend should be given time and space to grieve in peace. In our culture, we descend upon the home of the bereaved in large numbers and our grief is public. We are immediately surrounded by people we know and many we have never met before who insist on helping you in what way they can at this horrible time. A funeral is not a close family affair, it is more of a community event – for the first three days anyway, then there is silence. Then you are left in your own thoughts. Alone.

Following a death one weekend I accompanied Imran to pay our respects at the home of a family friend. Tucked away amidst the terraced streets was a small house and parking was difficult for most of the visitors and one driver in particular was struggling to get into a tight spot. It would have been easier to find somewhere more suitable, but the driver, who we recognised as Uncle Hakim, was insistent on squeezing into this spot. A small group of men watched as he slowly manoeuvred his vehicle into the space, eventually stopping centimetres short of the car behind. Having done something which I have to say was impressive for a man in his fifties, he got out of his car and looked at us. "Aasee ve Pakistan diya do rotian Khadian nay (Even I have eaten two rotees from Pakistan)."

It was a way of saying that he was in fact made of sterner stuff than the rest of us. Which I think he was.

Having entered the hallway of the house you would always be greeted by a mountain of shoes and the intelligent visitor would ensure he placed his footwear in a corner spot. Many a time someone had 'mistakenly' worn another man's shoes home only to return for the right pair.

We were crammed into a front room where the floor had been covered with a white sheet and sat knee to knee . It was a typical Asian household with Arabic calligraphy on the walls, flowered carpets and a single sofa, covered with a multi-coloured material. Another two-seater sofa had been balanced on its side so the room could accommodate more guests.

The mantelpiece had several images which had been placed facing down and the TV had been covered with another small sheet. A colourful camel, most likely brought from some back street in Pakistan, was stuffed behind a curtain in the corner.

Every so often people would enter the room and we would all raise our hands to say the customary prayers and respects would be paid to the relatives of the deceased. At times, the person walking in would scan the room as he had no idea to whom he should be paying his respects to. I mean, quite a few of us had been sent there on behalf of our parents to ensure the family was represented and had no idea who was related to whom. Thankfully, someone would nod in the direction of the person who should be offered the condolences.

There are those who would sit there silently in contemplation, but these types were few and far between – the majority would use this as an opportunity to discuss current affairs. If ever anyone really wanted to know what was going on in our town, one only needed to spend an hour in the company of these men and women, as I can imagine the same conversations were taking place in their section.

Now, I know some people spent as little time as possible at these gatherings, but I must admit there was much to be learned. Forget the polls, the reports and the studies – soon you would be up to date on everything there was to know, however insensitive that might sound.

At one house years earlier, I had sat and watched a man try to convince others that William Shakespeare had in fact been a Muslim. The bard had in fact been known to many as Sheikhs Pir and had travelled to the UK in the 1500s, and over time the British through their tradition of re-writing history had changed his name. His argument was pretty convincing at the time and I had spent an afternoon reading a Shakespeare biography.

Another time, two guests had almost come to blows outside over some altercation they had had a day earlier. This was of course rare as it would be very disrespectful to be bringing outside rivalries to the fore at a time like this.

It was also a time for people to make grand claims of what they could achieve if they were trusted with something. I had once heard Uncle Riaz promise that he could 'seat a passenger on a flying plane' – a feat which of course was impossible but it helped to convince others that he was a man of business and got things done.

Most times the conversation would take place in Punjabi and would inevitably turn to politics or religion. Today was no different, but not before the customary look at 'how we got here' discussion had been had.

"Amazing, isn't it," remarked Uncle Hakim studying a tatty Urdu magazine with a female driving a car pictured in it. "Over there they were picking up cow dung and here they want to drive."

In many rural Pakistani villages cow dung was collected, mostly by the women, dried on the walls and then used as fuel for the stove. "Give them an inch and they will take your whole house," he added.

"Did you ever say that to your wife, uncle?" asked Imran smiling.

"Do I look like someone who wants to have his throat slit in the middle of the night?"

This brought out more laughs than his earlier comment.

Imran wasn't content with letting Uncle Hakim get off so lightly. "You could say the same about you, uncle. You would be slogging it in the fields digging ditches but here you are watching your Sony TV."

I chuckled and then sensed there might actually be others in the room able to relate to this more than him. Uncle Hakim stroked his beard and felt Imran's observation did not warrant an answer and immediately turned his attentions to something more profound.

"The Indians are far more successful than us. You have to admit that. They have lower levels of crime and better mosques. We Pakistanis are falling behind in every way," said Uncle Hakim, having seated himself at what could only be described as the best spot in the room, right next to the heater.

Blackburn, like some surrounding towns, had a population that was made up of both descendants of Indian and Pakistani Muslims. The vast majority did not see any issues with this; others had used this on both sides to encourage subtle levels of prejudice whilst sat amongst their own. Up until the late eighties it also had several Hindu and Sikh families, but many had moved to the south.

Imran, unlike the rest of us, was not afraid to challenge such prejudices in public and was far more confident speaking in Punjabi in a group full of seniors. "I can't believe what I am hearing. Why would you say that?"

Whilst many people think themselves as being eloquent in both English and Punjabi, few can pull it off. Imran was a rare breed. He felt equally comfortable sat amongst some villagers as he would with the 'high society' types. Many of us will claim that we are comfortable in all surroundings but in reality, when the real questions are asked of us, we failed to convince.

"Just look around you," explained Uncle Hakim. "They are more organised than us. You know there is a story I got told back in the village – if you had five Pakistanis stuck in a hole none of them would ever get out. As soon as one reached the top, one of the other four would pull him back in. They would rather all suffer together than allow one to escape the hell hole."

It was, I have to say, an apt analogy and was one which was repeated at almost every gathering of this type. The aim was to show how we Pakistanis hated the fact that anyone else should be able to achieve anything of any significance.

Imran looked around the room. "You need to look at your own problems before you start making assumptions about other people I guess."

"They don't want to be associated with us," said Uncle Hakim. "They support their own businesses. When was the last time a Pakistani supported a Pakistani?"

"I wouldn't go that far," added Uncle Riaz. "We support one another all the time. I bought you that shalwar kameez with the secret pockets, didn't I?"

A small man with a white beard, Uncle Riaz was probably the wittiest man I had met who would find a quick-fire response to almost every argument and opinion there was. At a meeting like this he was in his element.

"No," said Uncle Hakim. "That is not the same. They make an effort to support each other in everything. We Pakistanis want the other guy to fail because we don't want to give him the attention or have to listen to others saying what a success he is. This is our downfall and always will be."

Several people nodded their heads in agreement and a couple got up from their seats and left. This had little to do with what Uncle Hakim had said, but people came and went like clockwork. I shifted my place several times so an elderly gentleman could be accommodated.

As someone entered the room prayers were said and as soon as those were out of the way the whispers and chatter would continue.

Imran was not convinced. "I think that is just what people use as an excuse to justify their own inconsistencies."

"Okay then," replied Uncle Hakim. "Why can't you get on to a committee of an Indian mosque? I will tell you why. They don't want you to be in a position of any power in their organisation. There is no difference between them and the goray who won't let us in positions of influence in the council."

This was a pretty loaded comment to make and one I had heard several times over the years. This notion that one set of Asians supported their own instilled further prejudice within smaller communities.

"That doesn't surprise me," added Uncle Riaz. "Why would they want you on any mosque committee? You would ruin it within months."

Everyone laughed. A teenager took out his mobile phone and began to type, making a beeping noise. "Look at this," noticed Uncle Hakim. "The only thing we are good at is playing with gadgets like this. Show me?"

He took the phone off the young man and turned it around and tried to remove the battery as the owner looked on nervously. "It's like a toy."

He handed the phone back to the teenager. "We need to be more like the Indians. They put Islam and deen (belief) first and then everything else after. It is the best way for our community."

Imran smiled and adjusted his seating position. "I think you will find that things are changing fast. This Indian-Pakistani thing is very much dated. People growing up now don't care about these things as much as you did. It is people like yourself who are sharing this ignorance, thus ensuring we never move on and the debate stays where it is."

Uncle Hakim attempted to win back the guests. "Why do they call us Paklos then?"

Again a few guests laughed, and I kept my head bowed hoping to hell I wasn't about to be involved in this discussion.

"Yes, and we call them Gujis," said Uncle Riaz.

A large gentleman in a beige shalwar kameez entered the room and attempted to squeeze himself into a small gap next to a table. He was struggling to take a seat. I always felt sorry for anyone who stood out a little walking into a room full of Punjabis as I knew full well someone would make a joke at his expense.

Uncle Riaz duly obliged. "Oh bhai just sit on the sofa. The floor was not made for you."

A few guests chuckled whilst another large gentleman in the corner blew his nose with a handkerchief and then wiped his brow with the same cloth.

Uncle Hakim glanced over at me and I was very much still hoping he would not drag me into this conversation. Unfortunately, I wasn't so lucky. "What do you think?"

I couldn't really be the silent observer anymore. "Well, I just think we have bigger problems to deal with than trying to score points against each other."

There was silence in the room and thankfully Imran intervened. "I think what he is trying to say is that we have a lot more to worry about and in the grand scheme of things and these things matter little when you are all trying to fight the wider system. If people don't want to work together to achieve something that's their problem, we don't all need to be like that."

Uncle Riaz nodded. "He said all that?"

Thankfully my contribution was interrupted by two more young men entering the room, one of whom was wearing ripped jeans and an Asian style shirt. "What happened to your pants, boy?" asked Uncle Riaz. "You get into a fight with a dwarf?"

The young man looked down sheepishly and laughed nervously. These types of gatherings were an opportunity to watch other people being demeaned for their looks and here was a prize candidate especially when he took his hoodie off to reveal a very short back and sides. It was cruel to see someone being ridiculed in this way but fun, nonetheless.

Imran came to the poor man's rescue. "Oh, uncle, leave him alone. It is today's style. I'm sure when you were younger you wore them flares and platform shoes."

Uncle Hakim laughed out loud. "Yes he did."

There was a lull in the conversation until Uncle Hakim began to pick at the skin on the soles of his feet and then flick them towards the bin.

Most days food would be served to guests but today none was forthcoming, which was a tad disappointing to some of the regulars whom I knew only visited the house at 'feeding time'. I had even personally spoken to some visitors who would criticise the standard of food served at a dead man's house.

Eventually Uncle Hakim decided to relay some more of his wisdom on the group. "You see this is the problem. We should be proud of wearing our national dress. These Indians have no national dress. Some wear jubbays and the others the kurtah and pyjama (Indian style dress). We can't even wear shalwar kameez properly anymore."

Even Imran had a resigned look on his face as he brushed his hair back.

"Can I ask you something, uncle?" said Imran. "You know when we go to an Indian's house to pay respects does anything like this happen?"

Uncle Hakim frowned. "What do you mean?"

"This. This talking about the world's current affairs and laughing and joking?"

There was silence in the room. "It doesn't," continued Imran. "That's because they realise that we have come to pay our respects and we should sit silently. We, on the other hand, try to find the next target to take the piss out of."

Again, there was silence, but thankfully normal service was resumed courtesy of Uncle Riaz: "Indians are better than us at everything then."

21 TAKE IT OR LEAVE IT

There was a race to get the first advert and it came from the unlikeliest of places. It didn't begin well but then when you are trying to persuade people to part with their hard-earned money things are never as easy as it looks.

Zak had dressed up the 'advertising game' but the reality was it was a hard slog. "You know in a few months we won't deal with these 'lallu panjus' anymore, we will be dealing directly with marketing agencies who will place all the major adverts and we will just have to book them over the phone."

Zak loved to sound so refined but at the same time used terms like 'Lallu panjus' in sentences. A 'lallu panju' was a term used only in our group to describe someone who thought a lot of themselves but in fact was as useful as a spoon at a Gujerati wedding.

It sounded so New York. Large advertising agencies placing corporate adverts in our lowly newspaper. "They all need to put an advert in to prove they are targeting 'hard to reach communities' and we will just sit back and sweep them up."

The reality is different.

One afternoon returning to Blackburn I had been driving with

Kal and visiting some businesses. "Check this place out."

We had driven out of our comfort zones and decided to stop at a carpet store hoping to land some adverts. "You really think this is a good idea?" I asked apprehensively.

"There is no harm in trying, is there. Advert is an advert no matter where you come from."

His faith in people was never dented, no matter where we went and who we met.

I puffed out my cheeks. "How about I wait here, and you go in."

Kal leaned over and took his folder from the back seat. "Come on, it will be fun."

How was this going to be fun? I really didn't want to do this. I think sales is a special type of job for a special type of person and I was not that person. "Nah, just leave it, Kal."

"Why are you being like this? Look, business is business and in business people are only interested in what you have to offer."

I agreed reluctantly and followed Kal into the building, which was a little more upmarket than the ones we had been visiting earlier.

A couple were in the showroom which was spacious compared to some of the other businesses we had wandered into.

"Hi, my name is Kal, can I speak to the owner of the business please." Kal was a lot more confident than me and a lot more forthright. No way would I have come into this place.

The man glanced up from his invoices. "Yes, that would be me."

"Okay, we are launching a new Asian newspaper and wondered if it might be something you would want to be featured in."

The woman who I presumed was his wife walked across the showroom and stood with her arms folded. "That's interesting. Will this paper be in English?"

"Yeah we get asked that a lot. It will be in English."

"We don't speak Asian here you know," she replied glancing across to her husband.

"Asian?" I said.

"Yes, whatever it is you speak."

Kal paused, put his pad down on the counter and smiled. "It isn't Asian, I can tell you that. We speak Punjabi or Urdu depending upon how we feel in the morning."

It seems we had got the husband's attention. "My next-door neighbours are great – they always make me a great curry for Christmas."

Kal glanced at me and I at him. "What has that got to do with the price of bread?"

"I was just saying that we like a good curry."

"Okay then."

There was an embarrassing silence as we tried to figure out whether to stay in the shop and try to sell the couple an advert or call it a day.

"Aren't you guys doing Ramadan at the moment?" the man asked.

There comes a part in every conversation when you wish they didn't bring up a subject like religion. The thing with religion is that any discussion can get personal and Kal was unlikely to be as patient as I had been.

"Yes, it is Ramadan – what of it?"

"It means you can't have sex."

It was at this point I realised that it was best we did in fact walk away, but Kal today was insistent that the conversation continue. "You can only have sex after sunset."

"That's a relief."

"It all depends if it was worth the wait," smiled Kal, and the couple laughed out loud and the mood changed almost instantly.

"So, this advert – are we doing it or what?" insisted Kal.

"Yeah okay, I suppose. Bring me the first issue after you print and we will talk."

Kal nodded his head and we both made our way of the store.

"You see," said Kal, "that wasn't too difficult at all. Once you get past the bullshit, anything is possible."

It was all too easy to gloss over blatant ignorance.

Kal loved to pretend he was far better off than he actually was, which was probably a way of saving face. Most of the time I would have to agree with him, but sometimes it was blatantly obvious he had been done over but he would still claim to be 50 pence up and it was funny to watch. The saying came from our games as kids when we would gamble with two pence pieces and at the end of the sessions Kal always came out with a profit. He was always 50 pence up.

It was Akeel who landed the first ever advert and it came from the local Midland Bank branch, which, despite being a multi-million-pound organisation, still bartered him down to £75. Soon enough the Eid messages were stacking up and Kal told Burger King that they should market their bean burger for 99p to Asians and Pizza Hut's

Sicilian pizza, 4 pieces of garlic bread and 1.5 litre bottle of Pepsi was an 'offer to die for'.

I had earlier headed off to Darwen Furniture Centre and met up with the owner who had taken up a quarter page advert on page two telling me, "I'm always up for trying something new. Let's give it go, shall we. Hopefully, we will get some of this stuff shifted."

It was so typically Lancashire I thought at the time. He had no idea who I was and had not even looked at the sheet of paper I was carrying around, but trusted me to deliver because I seemed like a 'nice chap'. More pertinently, he had not asked anything about it being an 'Asian' paper. This was Blackburn, or in this case, Darwen.

Despite these successes it was not going to be enough to print the newspaper never mind make any sort of profit.

Kal had come across Media Moguls, a PR agency based in London, and had immediately been impressed on the play on words. "That is one hell of name, isn't it?"

Zak had always felt it was more worthwhile for us to spend our time talking to mainstream companies.

"Asian businesses don't spend any money," said an exasperated Zak one evening as we sat in our favourite takeaway.

"That's quite a general comment, Zak," I said. "We can't be turning on our own. We got Univision Eye Centre, Cedar Street Food Store and Malik Travel Service. Major brands them for Blackburn." I felt extremely thankful to anyone who trusted me with their money.

Both Kal and Akeel had had their first shared experience of dealing with a local business and it had not gone too well. They had been hitting the shops along the popular Whalley Range of town.

Kal relayed the story to us as the 'chicken and chips' was served.

Akeel had introduced himself as they entered a local clothes store. "Could I interest you in this? We are launching a newspaper for Eid and maybe you would like to put an advert in?"

The store owner had mulled over the sheet and began to serve another customer. "How much?"

"Well we have three prices: £100, £175 and £300 for a full page."

The store owner had walked away and was gone for several minutes as Akeel and Kal stood there. Akeel was already losing patience. "What the fuck is this guy's problem?"

"Just relax," Kal had said. "He has probably gone to do some work or something."

The store owner then returned and sat down on his stool. "Okay, I give you £20 for one advert."

Kal smiled, hoping the man was joking. "We can't do it for that price."

It was a familiar tactic I had come across on my visits to some shops with some businesses stating ridiculous prices. And then the store owner had uttered the following words that incensed Akeel: "Take it or leave it."

'Take it or leave it' was a way of demeaning the other person and saying in no uncertain terms that you should get out of my store.

Kal was about to interject but Akeel had stopped him. "£20?" said an infuriated Akeel.

The store owner stood up from his seat and this time Kal had to interject. "I had to get Akeel out of there fast."

Akeel reminded him, "What the fuck, man? £20, Kal. What the hell are we going to do for £20. At least give me an offer I can play with."

"The guy was obviously above our pay grade," insisted Kal.

Akeel had then tried to lift bag of heavy flour on his way out. "Why don't we take this bag here—" but realised it was far too heavy. "In fact this much smaller, lighter bag for a pound – how would you like it?"

"That is for a pound," The store owner had replied.

"Wow, that is really good deal. How are you making any money?"

Kal couldn't wait to get out of the store. "He makes his money. Let's go."

Kal looked over at Akeel as he tucked into his fried chicken. "And what did you say when you left the place?"

"What did I say?"

"For £20 you wouldn't let him wipe your arse."

I laughed and then turned to Akeel. "Come on, Aki. If you are going to make a grand exit at least say something that makes sense."

Akeel had a confused look on his face. "It made complete sense to me."

22 T-BONE

"We should come up with story ideas," I proposed.

You would think that stories just appear and we put them together and print them. It was easier than it sounded. It was slowly dawning on us that journalism required us to go out and chase down actual stories. That was essentially the nature of the job. Getting adverts to support the paper was tough, but at least we knew who and where these people were.

It was Friday night so we treated ourselves to our favourite chicken and chips in the office.

"Eid on two days?" Zak blurted out.

"A bit predictable," I said. "How about middle-class Asian gangster mummy's boys and their girlfriends?"

"Daytime Bhangra Do's" said Kal.

"They still do those?" I asked.

"I don't know. Maybe," said Zak.

Sitting around this so-called newsroom was driving us a little crazy but it did give us time to mull over plans and ideas. I sat with my feet on the desk again whilst Kal had his familiar pose with his hands under his chin. Zak was back flicking through that damn Filofax.

Zak scratched his head. "The best kebab roll in Blackburn?"

"Paradise Chippy," I said.

"K2 Chippy?" said Kal.

"No way. Rusholme Chippy," I replied.

Zak shook his head. "Which is in Manchester. Can we get back to the subjects at hand please?"

"Asians in football," I said.

"And?" asked Kal.

"There are no Asians in football?" I said.

"Interesting," added Zak and began to take notes. "Okay we can hold that one."

"Perverts, "I shouted out.

"Go on?" said Kal.

"Nothing. Just perverts." I laughed.

There was a silence.

"Okay I got it," I piped up again. "Guys who wear brown shalwar kameez are decent whilst guys who wear sky blue shalwar kameezes turn out to be nutters. Whenever there is a fight you always see a sky blue shalwar in the middle of it all."

Kal seemed a little more concerned that we did not have any tangible ideas. "This is all not helping at all. We can't just make things up and print them. What does a real newspaper do?"

Zak scratched his head and folded his arms. "They make things up and print them."

Akeel walked in and sat down. I got him up to speed on what may or may not constitute an idea for a story.

"Okay, I got one this one woman call earlier, says that the family are not letting her get married to the guy because her boyfriend is Pakistani?"

"Not our problem?" said Zak.

"What do you want me to say?" I said.

Akeel intervened. "We aren't relationship counsellors, are we. We are a bunch of guys sitting in a toilet paper factory trying to print a newspaper about real social issues affecting the young people of our town."

I glanced at Akeel. "It is a social issue facing the young people of our town. Love across the divides."

Kal had other ideas. "I can speak to her and set her straight. Tell her to wake up and stop living in some Bollywood movie. The happy couple do not walk off into the sunset and live happily ever after. It is miserable and life is shit and in the end the bastards WILL grind you down."

We all looked at Kal with worried expressions. "Okaaay, probably not what we want to tell her… just yet."

"So, you are going to lie to her?" said Kal.

Zak intervened. "It is not our responsibility to deal with people's personal issues. Not our problem. We are a newspaper."

I wasn't about to let this go. "But as a newspaper maybe we should be dealing with this?"

"How? How can we deal with this? Are you going to go round to the guy's house to speak to the dad?" said Kal.

"No," I said.

"So, there is nothing else we can do. Forget about this."

Zak looked across from his pad and wrote another few words down and then crossed them out. "Okay then, how about we do a feature on racism."

"Racism where?" said Akeel.

"I don't know, there must be some racism somewhere we can tap into?" added Zak with that same deadpan look on his face.

To say I wasn't shocked at what he just said would be an understatement. "We can't just tap into racism? It doesn't work that way. Either there is racism or there isn't – we don't just invent racism for the sake of it to fill some pages."

"Why not?" asked Zak.

I was visibly shocked even though I knew Zak was joking. "Because it doesn't work that way! Making racism up is the most unethical thing anyone can do. We can't just accuse people of being racist for the sake of it."

"He's joking, Shuiaby. Of course, no one is going to do that," said Kal as Zak smiled.

Maybe I had misjudged Zak's initial comment. "But there is racism around, isn't there? Between Pakistanis and Indians."

And there you had it. Zak wanted us to publish and be damned from the very first issue. "So, we are going to ignore the whole Pakistani-Indian thing?"

I was hoping for some support from Kal and Akeel, but it wasn't forthcoming. I think they had decided that this was an argument not even worth getting into. "No, I didn't say that. What I am saying is we print it but let's not make a big issue of out of it."

"Why?" said Zak.

"Because none of that actually matters, does it. Pakistanis, Indian, Bengalis, we are all still going through the same shit as we were ten years ago."

The door opened and Imran made his way into the room; I welcomed him with open arms. "Mr Imran, glad you could join us. These guys are taking us into some fucked up place from where there will be no redemption."

Imran ignored my advances. "How's the paper doing?"

"Okayish," I replied. "We were just discussing whether we should write about Pakistanis and Indians not getting along."

"Who says they don't get along?"

"Zak here, seems to think we are a bunch of raging racists and Kal wants to break some poor girl's hopes of getting married."

Imran had not been able to contribute as much as he would have wanted to in the past few days but when he did make a point it was worth waiting for. "I think maybe you guys are thinking about this all wrong. At this moment in time you don't know what is and what is not important. You won't find out until you print the newspaper and it hits the streets."

"Go on," said Kal.

"Presently, what do you actually know about what is going on? You haven't really got a clue. You think you know but you don't. We know we as a community have issues with drug abuse, racism and barriers to employment. All these things will be something we tackle in the next year. At the moment we need to get this paper out."

I got up again and placed my hand on Imran's shoulder. "You see, THIS is the reason we are related. We will take your opinions on board at the next editorial meeting. Which is actually now. Motion passed."

Imran laughed out loud.

We spotted bright car headlights shine through the only window onto the office wall.

"Who is that?" I looked at everyone. "Anybody?"

Kal checked his phone. "It's T-bone. He needs some bog rolls. I better deal with him."

Now, T-bone, real name Mumtaz, ran his own cash and carry business but had problems with alcohol.

"There's an idea, Zak, Bastard Sharabees (alcoholics)," I explained.

"What?"

"You know T-bone? Top fellow but he is one of those guys who when he's had a few on Eid becomes a really mean son of a bitch. A proper harami (a total savage) of the highest order."

Zak laughed. "Sign him up – he would fit right into journalism. What colour shalwar kameez does he wear?"

I paused. "Strangely enough he wears a sky blue one."

23 CARRY ON CLEO

"We can't put anything about sex in an Asian newspaper." I looked over at the other two in the office, expecting both to agree.

"Why not?" said Zak who tonight was wearing a three-piece suit for some reason. I mean no disrespect to our office and surroundings, but he looked as out of place as a bacon sandwich at a Muslim wedding.

The office was unusually hot tonight as we sat around contemplating a subject we had been skirting around. What type of newspaper did we want to be? And where would we draw the line? And what would be deemed offensive and what would be seen as acceptable to our audiences?

There are certain things you can talk about and there are other topics you would rather not bring up. One of those was what was referred to in some circles as 'dirty stuff'. Even the word 'sex' left some of us in palpitations when uttered in front of older family members.

Whilst we would like to think we were the liberal types, in our hometown we were just as prudish as everyone else. Talking about sex in an Asian paper would invite the wrong sort of attention, so would it not be best to avoid it altogether?

"We just can't," I said. "It will get us into trouble."

Kal was not dressed as impeccably as Zak and was scrolling through some sheets on his desk. "Zak's right, why not? If there is a story about sex, then it has to go in, doesn't it? I'm sure we are past them days."

It wasn't the answer I had been expecting, "Yeah I suppose. But 'no' we can't do that. People accept many things, but SEX is not one of them."

It was one of those subjects that still caused embarrassment to some people, as we didn't know exactly who those readers were at this stage, I thought it best to avoid any criticisms. Both Zak and Kal didn't seem to realise what the fuss was about. "Look, we can't change them. They are just so coy about it," I explained. "Come on, you guys clam up when Sid James laughs!"

Sid James' laugh had been a standard bearer on levels of obscenity ever since we were kids and it was always a good yardstick to begin with. Just hearing that laugh meant something salacious had happened or was about to take place. Whenever a Carry On movie was being aired in our households, someone had to sit right next to the TV to change the channel in case Barbara Windsor had one of her 'mishaps'.

Zak recollected, "You can't knock Carry On movies. My favourite was Carry on up the Khyber. Even the title has filthy connotations."

"It has?" asked a confused Kal.

"Yeah, you know Carry On UP the Khyber."

I frowned. "I thought the Khyber meant the Khyber. Oh, I see.

Yeah Khyber."

Zak seemed almost delighted to be sharing his theory with us. "Carry On Screaming, Carry On Up The Jungle, Carry On Follow That Camel, Carry On Don't Lose Your Head. All filth. I mean I don't even know how they got away with it."

I glanced over at Kal. "No, I don't think…" I thought about it. "Oh yeah, could be, couldn't it?" I paused again. "Anyway, it just won't work in this paper. We just aren't ready for this."

We sat there silently pondering Zak's observations on Carry On titles. I could not see why these two continued to entertain something that would invite more criticism that it was worth. It was always better to be safe on these matters. The last thing we wanted was some guy calling us some sort of deviants.

Even consenting couples would go to a great deal of trouble not to be spotted with one another. The idea of being seen with someone from the opposite sex anywhere was probably one of the most degrading things that could happen to an Asian couple. Much of the time the meeting could well be innocent, but walking through a park was fraught with danger. One moment the couple were together, and the next ten feet apart. It was a skill one picked up and could not be taught.

The library was a firm favourite for some, and I do recollect only weeks earlier speaking to one father who said his son was studying hard and always in the library. 'He particularly likes the reference section on the top floor,' I told his proud dad.

Other couples would go to great lengths to hide their

misdemeanours from their relations, which was far easier said than done, especially as some people had 'extended extended family members'. The amount of detailed planning that went into concealing one's relationship from anyone who may later use it against the family at a dinner party would impress a secret agency. Parents would also use code language of their own to conceal the fact their sons were in a relationship – "That's his 'friend'."

Zak was more optimistic. "It's 1997... I mean 1998. I think people are responsible enough now to talk about sex. There are a lot of problems we could raise and a lot of these are related to sex and relationships."

Clearly, many communities had ignored these issues and the burgeoning younger populations were slowly breaking away from these misconceptions. But our town was different.

Kal finally agreed. "Thinking about it now, no we will get lynched."

"Look, our paper is hardly going to be a DH Lawrence novel, is it?" said Zak. "But it would be good to get the odd story in."

There was another one of those silences in the office. "Okay, what if the story warrants sexual language?" asked Zak.

"It won't," I said abruptly.

Kal put his hands under his chin, something he tended to do when he was going to say something profound and was having reservations on his earlier comment. "It might? What if we have a story that means we have to use a so-called dirty word?"

This was going to be something we had to think about, and it was best to avoid any misunderstanding.

I got up from my seat and paced around the small room and sat back down. "Then we just don't use the dirty word, we use something else that means dirty. For instance, instead of sex we can say 'intimate'."

"Intimate?" said Zak.

"Yeah the couple were getting intimate. It is so much nicer. It is the kind of thing respectable, nice couples do."

Zak looked at me more confused than before. "What if we can't use the word 'intimate' and it requires another more daring word?"

If there was one thing I could rely on, was Zak wanting to push boundaries and test someone else's patience.

I sighed heavily. "Then we will find another phrase. Like 'they got together' or they 'met on mutual terms' and both 'parents were happy'."

Zak spun his phone around on his desk. "Okay then, how would we report the Monica Lewinsky scandal? There has to be some sex in there doesn't there?"

"Well then." I paused. "We wouldn't report on it because they aren't an Asian couple, and we are only reporting Asian news."

Kal was sat switching his lighter on and off and now had other concerns. "What about if a brother gets caught at a 'dogging spot'?"

I nodded my head, stood up again, taking a cigarette from my pocket and took hold of Kal's lighter. "That's a tough one. Well then, we will just have to say he should have known better."

The idea of replacing terms we thought might be prudish and offensive would make our lives less problematic.

"That makes no sense. We can't possibly keep the word sex…" began Kal.

"Ah aha ah, 'intimate relationship'," I interrupted.

Kal was still a little puzzled. "I mean sex okay. Sex sex sex. This might not be the time for it, but we can't keep the word 'sex' out of the paper forever."

He was right of course but I wasn't about to give up just yet. "If people can keep it out of their relationship then we can damn right keep it out of the paper."

Zak chuckled.

"Anyway, if you include sex in the paper, we won't be able to distribute in the mosques and people's homes. I can imagine it now – 'This dirty paper has sex in it so it must be haram' and 'Don't let your daughters read this filthy rag' and so on and so forth. If you know something is going to cause you problems, then why not sidestep it?"

That stopped them in their tracks.

Zak wasn't finished. "But that is society. It is everywhere. It is part of people's lives. We just ban it completely? If we start censoring stuff, then we are no better than the rest of them. I thought we were meant to be different."

But we could. We could ban it.

It would be best to describe my understanding of censorship. "Okay, you know in an Indian movie when a couple are together, when things are about to get clever what do they show?"

Zak and Kal both shrugged their shoulders. "I don't know... a cucumber?" said Kal.

"Good guess but maybe not the type of Indian movie the rest of us watch. No, they show a flower. You know it is nice. It is pure, it is lovely. It signifies something has happened, but we don't know EXACTLY what has happened. That way Auntie Jee in her headscarf is comfortable watching the movie alongside her son, daughter and the neighbour's cat."

Zak laughed out loud. "In a Carry On movie they show a train entering a tunnel."

"Yes," I explained. "But that is because they are British, and they invented the steam train. The British show trains entering tunnels; we show orchids. Or in our case we are just going to say intimate relations."

We heard the outside door opening and footsteps. Akeel entered the room and looked at us all. "What the fuck is going on here then?"

"Shuiaby won't let us use sex in the paper," said Kal.

"What? Gay sex?" replied Akeel.

"Woah woah woah!" I stood up again. "No, just sex. Gay sex? I don't have a term for that yet. Any suggestions?"

Everyone looked down in silence.

24 FOOTBALL

I felt sorry for my sisters who had to put up with four brothers who were football mad.

With one television there was always going to be problems when major tournaments came round. If there is one thing I could not understand, even as a kid, was why people would just turn up at the door unannounced. It was a very Asian thing to do. When both parents were not home one of us would have to sit in the front room and make polite conversation with some bloke. We felt guilty and the bloke seemed genuinely upset. Other times with the door being left open Auntie-Jee would stroll in with her entourage whilst one was having a snooze on the sofa.

It caused havoc during the World Cup. In the 1986 World Cup quarter-final between France and Brazil and the game locked at 1-1, a family turned up at my house 'unannounced'. Whilst my mother let them in and politely sat them down, I huddled next to the TV to watch the rest of the match, only to be drawn away every few minutes to complete some chores. I was rude and I was agitated, and at the time I thought it was deeply troubling that this family – and in particular the man of the house – had not realised there was a

World Cup quarter-final being played on the day. Had he not heard of Socrates or Platini? What kind of man takes his family to someone else's home at a time like this? And it seemed lightning does strike twice. On the final day of the Premier League campaign in 1995 and with Blackburn Rovers leading 1-0, a whole party of 'family friends' decided it would be a good day to visit the Khans. I ended up listening to much of the second half from a car radio two streets away.

Football was everything. For many of us growing up in this town, football was the only thing of any importance and most of all it gave us something to do. If you didn't play football or follow cricket, then you could well be ostracised, so even those who were rubbish at it made an effort to take part.

The past decade we had cheered Pakistan to a World Cup victory and watched England lose on penalties twice to the same opposition. Something that seemed to greatly bother Zak and Benny, who were insistent that we support England both in cricket and football.

But we couldn't do that.

The fact was many of us still supported Pakistan because it was a way of sticking two fingers up at the non-existent empire. Cricket was in many ways a sport that defined Asians in this country. You could be proudly patriotic but as soon as you crossed that boundary, we hated the English with a vengeance. Much of this had to do with how cricket was perceived. It was a timely reminder about how the English had introduced the sport to the natives and these village folk had got better at it than them. The press were also vehemently racist towards the Indians and the Pakistanis, and I would read countless articles of how 'our precious England' was being cheated by these new masters of in-swing bowling.

I am sure many Englishmen could not understand why so many British-born Asians supported the country of their forefathers. It was simple. For a moment, and just for that one moment, we felt like our immigrant fathers, on the other side, and cricket with its high society roots was the perfect opportunity to turn back the clock.

In this town, to keep yourself occupied you had to play football or cricket. As a kid kicking the ball around on Lancaster Place, our game was interrupted one afternoon by two brothers who had moved in at the end of the road. We picked sides and the moments that followed are still etched in my memory. One brother was the most breath-taking player we had seen: he was quick, he was strong and it was hard not to applaud every time he placed the ball into the top corner of the red brick wall. Soon enough we noticed how his younger brother would wave at him every so often to get his attention and as the game drew to a close we huddled round to congratulate this amazing footballer, who remained strangely silent. His brother who was no more than nine years old at the time began by telling us the name of his older sibling and revealed to us his brother was deaf. It was the beginning of a childhood friendship that lasted for many years. Many football games passed, but never did I ever see a more accomplished footballer.

I was involved in football several times a week and the most enjoyable was a seven-a-side league which took place on a Friday night. It was made up predominantly of Asian teams who fought week in week out to have the bragging rights. Our team, named Bank Top Rovers, had real swagger about it at times because it had a great mix of young and older players who played some entertaining football. Our nemeses were Comet FC and a team in green named Whalley Range who always found a way to beat us and everyone else in the league. It was a valuable lesson that you could look pretty and play some fantastic football but if you wanted to win anything then you needed to have some grit about you. Pretty football may be good to watch, but you can't win leagues with fancy football and entertaining players.

Football was also a unifying force in towns like ours. Despite what happened off the pitch, on it we were all the same. It didn't make any difference who you were, but on the pitch you were just another player. Yes, it was shit some days, but footballers are a funny bunch – we were more likely to ridicule one's hair and weight than one's colour as long as that brother was on our side.

Not once in the first few weeks of our new venture did anyone worry about how to cover sport. We knew about sport and we knew it all too well.

Wouldn't it be great if someone was to come here on the side of the pitch and take some pictures of Asians playing amateur football I had always thought. So, we did.

25 JAFFA CAKES

Sales is all about persuading someone to buy something they may not actually need. Advertising as we had learned is about persuading someone to buy some blank space in the hope it will benefit their own business. It was as simple as that.

A free newspaper is very different from a paid-for title. A free newspaper does not get printed unless you raise more money than it costs to print that edition. You are playing catch up from the very first moment you decide to print an issue. So, making that all-important sale was the difference between success and failure.

But then there were times when you didn't need to make a sale. It was presented to you on a plate. All you had to do was get the order form signed and lie back, content that you had done a hard day's work.

Or so we thought.

Another day and another frustrating time trying to convince people to advertise in something they had not yet seen.

This was a tough business to be in.

Kal was sat at the office one evening flicking through a Yellow Pages to study which businesses we could target for some more advertising. It had become a thankless task at times, and we were beginning to tire of the constant rejection in pursuit of our make-or-break target.

Kal's phone began to ring. "Hello… Hello… HELLLLOOOO." He flipped the phone shut. "Crap reception here sometimes."

Kal had earlier received a call from a gentleman who wanted to place an advert. "What did that guy say? Is he coming in?"

"Yes, he said he would pop over at 7.30." There was a loud knock on the outside of the shutter door. "This could be him. Are you going to get him?".

Whenever we had a guest one of us would pretend to act as if we were the personal assistant to the boss. Today was my turn. I hurried out into the car park and spotted a man banging loudly on the wrong door. I called over to him and ushered him into the office.

The smallish man with thick hair was wearing a smart suit; he sat down in front of Kal and gazed around the office.

He introduced himself as Musa, a businessman, who wanted to advertise in the newspaper. "I think this is a really wonderful thing you guys are doing for the community. People need something that will speak up for our rights and help businesses."

I sat down across the room and thought it best that Kal close this deal. We had an unspoken rule between us that if one of us was speaking to someone, it would be rude if the other interjected unless invited to do so.

After what had been a difficult day, Kal looked pleased. "That is very kind of you. We thought the town could benefit from a newspaper like ours. There are so many success stories in this town that just don't get told and we really need to be able to talk about ourselves more."

"I agree." Musa looked at back at me. "If we don't help each other then who will help us? I do hope this is a big success and I will be telling some of my friends who own businesses too to advertise."

Kal gestured over to me and then asked the man, "Would you like some tea?"

"Oh yes, that would be lovely."

"Sugar?" I walked over to the small kitchen area. "And milk?"

"Yes, two sugars and milk will be fine."

Kal didn't like wasting too much time and I could hear him telling Musa about the factory and how this office was just temporary, and we would be moving into a larger place later. He went on to talk about the toilet roll business too and I could hear laughter.

Regardless of how homely the place felt it was still an office in a factory and not exactly a newsroom.

The day had been particularly tough for us. It was Ramadan. Quite a number of businesses remained shut and we had not had much luck calling potential customers.

It was wonderful, I thought to myself. Here we were at the end of the day just about to give up and in walked this kind gentleman. Our luck was in.

"So, this newspaper of yours, it is free?" asked Musa.

"Yes, it is."

I placed a cup of tea in front of the man and another in front of Khalil. Musa slurped his tea and complimented me.

Kal got down to business. "So, how can we help you today? You said on the phone you wanted to book some adverts."

Musa was forthright and to the point. "I would like to place six adverts if I may. Can you do me a full page each month?"

Kal looked over to me and pretending not to be completely overtaken by what he had heard. Six months! A full page each month! This is just what we needed today.

Kal gazed over at me again. "Shuiab, have you got any of that cake?"

Cake? I would cook the man a biryani if he wanted one.

I hurried across to the kitchen and brought a chocolate cake we had been saving for special occasions. Placing it in front of both men, I cut it into large pieces. Eat, my dear friend. Eat the cake.

"That is wonderful, thank you both. You are too kind. You two really know how to spoil people."

"Oh, it's okay," said Kal. "It is great of you to come down at this hour. You know you just made our day. So then, what will you need to place in your advert?"

Musa removed a large A4 sheet from an envelope he had been holding. This was getting better – we wouldn't even have to design the advert. Anyone working in an advertising sales office will tell you – a completed advert is the most wonderful thing you can present to a representative. It saves you having to produce endless amounts of proofs to be checked over and over again until the client it happy.

He handed Kal the advert, who was now looking even more pleased with himself and gestured to me again. "Shuiab, have you got any of those Jaffa Cakes?"

Only the best for our new best friend I thought. Jaffa Cakes it is.

I placed the half-open pack in front of the man who took a biscuit out and dunked it into his tea.

"Oh, nice, you dunk your Jaffa cakes."

Musa laughed.

You know things are not that bad. People are generally good and just when you think it is time to give up god will give you a sign. This was the happiest I had been for a while and I kind of forgot what a horrible day it had been. The cosmic forces that bind us all were now working in our favour.

Kal had been busy calculating the prices and printing off an order sheet. "Okay then, sir, I have the order sheet here if you want to have a quick look and just check if everything is fine."

Musa stared at the sheet and pointed at the price. "I just want to check." He hesitated. "Is there a cost to this?"

Kal looked up at him and then at me and then back at him. "Yes."

Musa gazed at me and then back at Kal. He then uttered five words that were etched into memory for all time: "I thought it was free."

I slumped back into my chair. I didn't even want to look at Kal who was sat right in front of Musa. But then, like a small child peering from behind a sofa trying to watch a horror movie, I raised my head slightly to stare at Kal.

He had the face of a goalkeeper who had just conceded two goals in the final minutes of a cup final.

Kal leaned forward and put both his hands on the desk. "Why would it be free?"

Musa seemed oblivious to the pain and anguish he had inflicted on us. "Well, you said it was a free Asian newspaper. So, I thought adverts were free for Asians."

I still didn't have the heart to say anything and looked at Kal for some guidance. He sat back in his chair and then stared at Musa dunking his third Jaffa Cake into his tea. "No, the paper is free, the paper. There is no cost to the paper; it does not mean the adverts are free. Come on."

Kal was not good at hiding his emotions when faced with an injustice. I got up from my seat and sat on the edge of desk. "It is okay, Bhai Saab. Don't worry about it. Anyone could make that mistake."

Kal was still sat back in his seat. It had not turned out to be a good day at all.

I paced over and picked up the remaining pack of Jaffa Cakes and smiled at Musa. "Good biscuits these, aren't they?"

Musa looked up apologetically and nodded his head.

26 THE SUIT

Some people like to draw attention to themselves and others don't. I was never someone who liked to draw attention to myself. None of us were. This had little to do with being humble if I am going to be honest, but more due to the fact there was no real need to boast about your meagre achievements. It was far more important at this stage to just get on with the job.

Two weeks in and my brother collared me one morning as he'd decided he wanted to buy me a suit. It was a three-piece suit complete with a waistcoat which was the fashion at the time. I stole a few ties from my other brother and decided this was my new look for now. You can't be a businessman if you don't look like a businessman.

As we couldn't hold a meeting anywhere during the day, we would end up meeting in Zak's front room.

I walked across to his house and into his front room where both Kal and Zak were sat. "Hey, look at this guy," said Zak.

"Are you getting married?" said Kal. "Where did you get the suit from?"

I nodded my head and turned my head to the side as if posing on a catwalk. "My brother got it from Top Man. As in my real bother not you semi-brothers. I don't know, I think he probably thinks if he gets me a suit I will move out of the house and stop dipping into his saag (spinach).

"See this pocket here," gesturing to the waistcoat, "this is for my pocket watch. Yes, I am getting a pocket watch for myself. And maybe a hat. Do we still wear hats?"

Kal and Zak laughed. "Why don't you get a tangah (horse and carriage) too and see if they can pull you up Bromley Street."

Bromley Street was the steepest street in Blackburn.

"I only popped in to see you guys. I have a meeting with a Mr Mason at Blackburn College. He is the marketing manager there. Wish me luck. If this suit doesn't work, then I have nothing else. Today, I am the suit."

Heading off to the meeting I felt a little more confident about the day. I had called and set up the meeting only two days earlier.

The marketing team (or one individual) was based in an old part of the Victoria building and the office was a little difficult to find. When you have so much relying on the meeting and you can't find the office, a level of panic sets in. I asked two people who eventually pointed me towards a small room at the top of the stairs. I knocked on the door and entered, to see a smartly dressed man leant back in his chair.

He was surrounded by reams of paper and the room itself looked like it could have done with a clean.

"Mr Mason, is it?"

"Hello, Shuiab… did I say that right?"

"Yes, it is pronounced Shu-aib. My father got the 'I' and the 'A' the wrong way round when he registered me, so it is Shu-aib. But what you said was correct."

That was a good sign. At school they had pronounced the name as Shu-ab, which was totally incorrect but once you get past the first year you stop caring.

I handed him the familiar A4 sheet I was carrying around.

"So, what is this then?"

"It is a new newspaper we are publishing. And here we have the sizes and the prices. You have £150 for the quarter page and… well so on and so forth."

He smiled politely. "I am well aware of advert sizes for newsprint. No, I didn't mean to be rude but yes, I see the sizes. You don't have a newspaper to show me yet though?"

"Oh no. Nothing – this is it at the moment. We print for Eid, I mean on Eid. For Eid."

"Looks very good. This has got potential. How much do you want?"

Now, this kind of took me off guard as it was the first time someone had taken such an interest in what I was selling. "It depends on what type of advert you want?"

"Let's go for the front page, shall we."

"Well let me check the price… It comes in at £300."

"Okay done. £300."

"Oh. Okay. Great thanks."

"And here is what I want writing. Logo and Eid Mubarak. Invoice me on this address."

I scribbled down a few notes and then handed him an order sheet to sign.

"And Shuiab. Drop me a few copies here afterwards. I would like to have a read."

"Thanks. Brilliant. Okay, I shall see you soon then."

"Great. Have a good day."

"Yes, you too, sir. I mean Paul."

There was something magnificent about having some good news to tell the others. Later in the day I walked into our makeshift office.

"Ladies, gentlemen and those who profess to be both, let me introduce you to the man who sold the front page."

Kal was holding two cups of tea. "No way."

"Yes way."

"Who the hell did you sell it to?"

I pulled out my sheet and slammed it on the table.

"There, read it and weep. That's better than having Shabba Ranks, Maxi Priest and Shaukat Ali play at your wedding."

It was time to revel in my moment of glory. "Blackburn College. Monsieur Paul. Top man. Me and Paul Bhai are going to be good friends one day. I have to say, the guy was really polite."

Kal seemed to be impressed. "Brilliant. You done good, Khan. Very good. Front page. Looks like that suit worked. From now on you should be wearing it morning, noon and night. In fact, sleep with the suit on."

I sat down and placed both my hands on the armrest. "I think I might. This is a powerful suit. You know I don't think I have ever sold anything to anyone. Apart from that time me and Kal were selling them VHS tapes."

"Oh aye!" remarked Zak.

"No not those type of tapes," I said. "These were blank tapes and we went door to door to sell them. You remember, Kal."

Kal laughed. "That one bloke who bought everything in our bag."

"Yeah then he realised he didn't even have a video player."

27 WOMEN'S STUFF

Something was missing from the very first day.

Here was the problem. Anywhere else we would have been able to simply call up a female friend and ask her if she wanted to work for a newspaper. However, *we* could not. It would be frowned upon to have a female in this newsroom in a community like ours. A toilet factory office in the backstreets of Blackburn was not exactly the kind of place to invite anyone.

So, it was time to face up to our predicament.

"Don't you think this is a little too male-orientated? This newspaper I mean. We need jannanee (women) stuff to make the janannian read it," I said one evening as we studied our page plan.

If we wanted to publish content for women, it would help if we had some female reporters.

Kal agreed. "Yes, I suppose we could do with some. You know any women?"

"No. Do you?" I asked.

Zak, however, had other ideas and didn't think it necessary at all. "Listen we don't need any women. We can write it all. What do we need women for? Far too many decisions to make and nothing will get done."

It was the kind of comment that was all too familiar within our circle of friends.

"That's a bit sexist even for you."

"It's true. Imagine a woman in here right now. Half of you will be arguing with her and the other half will be trying to get into her pants."

Kal glanced at me. "Some of us will be doing both."

It was something we would have to deal with at a later date. "I'm glad there are no women in here. I am not good with women. Never have been. I find them far too complicated. They always make me do shit I don't want to."

"It is because you put them on a pedestal," Zak advised.

Kal looked towards me again and joked, "You can't behave like a jananee (woman) with a jananee. You have to be a jannah (man)."

It made sense to me. "I am a Jannah. I find the whole process extremely stressful. I would ideally like a jananee who behaves like a Jannah. You know, lets me play football and watch football, but at the same time behaves like a woman."

Kal had been adding up some figures on a calculator and punched some more numbers in. "You want a Jannah-jananee!"

"Exactly, like Amitabh says in Naseeb," I said.

Zak glanced up from the screen. "That is not what it means."

I think we had gone off track, but it was a common theme. "I know. But I need a woman who is really a man. Okay, that sounds completely wrong, but you know what I mean."

Zak laughed. "Is there something you want to share with us?"

Every few days a driver would make his way into the office to pick up the odd rolls on a late run. Raheem, a stocky man with a centre parting, opened the door and stood next to Kal and began to exchange sheets.

I leant back in my chair and put my feet back on to the desk. "We do need some female news in here and we can't do it with guys like us. We don't really know what makes a woman tick. What they are interested in? What bothers them?"

Raheem turned his attention to me. "What about period news?" and then stared at Kal.

There was awkward silence in the room.

Zak swivelled his chair around to face Raheem. "I don't even know what to say to that."

"A monthly update for menstruating women," added Raheem with that same blank expression.

Zak refused to be drawn in. "Still, I don't know what to say to that."

"How to get some action when…" Raheem was interrupted by Zak. "Woah let me stop you there. Okay, that is enough. We can't discuss this – it is illegal. It must be illegal. I think we can be arrested for this or something. There must be a law against men discussing women's stuff and if there isn't there should be."

Raheem laughed and walked out of the office.

We sat there silently. I looked at Kal again, contemplating if he was about to add to Raheem's clearly stupid idea.

We could not print a new 'modern newspaper' for the Asian community and tell only one side of the story. Otherwise, we would be doing exactly the same as everyone else.

Kal stood up again and paced around the office. "How do the big newspapers do this? All these men writing about women's issues. They must know something we don't? There must be a trick to this? It can't be that hard."

"They don't. They just put a model on the front page," said Zak.

"Isn't that a bit shit really? What is the point of that?" I asked.

"Yeah, but it sells papers, doesn't it? Put a pretty picture on the cover alongside some hard news."

I looked up at the other two. "It is a man thing, isn't it? If all else fails we just bang a woman on the front page."

Kal laughed. "Yeah… that'll do." And laughed again.

I frowned at Kal. "I don't even know why that it is funny?"

"Oh, yes it is," and he sniggered again.

We were going way off track again. "Zak, how did you get round this last time?"

Zak had that expression on his face. The type he had when he was about to say something really inspiring.

"Well," he paused. "What we did was – and this might not be to everyone's taste – we pretended to be women."

This wasn't what I was expecting and coming from someone who was always keen to put us in our place whenever anyone made overtly sexist comments I was a little shocked. "Okay, I honestly thought you were going to give us some real insight into journalism. That's just bollocks."

Kal was making some tea in the corner by now. "Let him finish."

Zak paused again. He did like to build up some suspense sometimes. Other times it was just frustrating.

"Well, you just put a by-line in of a woman."

"What's a by-line again?" asked Kal.

"It is the name at the top of the article. Is that allowed?" I said.

"Why not? Everyone does it" explained Zak. "Who's to know you are not a woman? It is like Zaika Akkas, but you have to write the words, I'm afraid, and be a woman. So, you have to know about female issues and really know what they are about. It requires research and actual work."

I looked over at Kal. "So, it is just cross-dressing but without the actual clothes?"

Zak tried to give a level of credibility to his idea. "I suppose it is. But you can't put any old shit in as you will get found out. You have to really know what a woman is about. People aren't stupid. They will know straight away if a bloke has written it. And it can't come across patronising in any way either. Also, I know we joke a lot but you have to cut that shit out."

I am sure it had been attempted many a time before, but I wasn't too sure about Zak's claim that 'everyone did it'.

Kal was convinced. "How hard can it be? You just write a story about women's issues and pretend to be a woman. And if anyone asks, we will say she is not available. Nobody is going to ask anyway. Nobody cares. We are hardly the Daily Mirror."

I gave Kal a concerned look. "What the fuck do you know about women's stuff?"

Zak intervened. "It is fine. We know enough to get by."

There was a slow realisation that we were simply making things up as we went along.

I put both my hands behind my head and gazed at the ceiling. "Okay, Kal, start writing that period news story."

28 DOESN'T IT

Having established our roles, the newspaper was quickly taking shape. We were well off our monetary target but decided to have a mini celebration late in the evening at a takeaway anyway.

It was getting late and Kal, Zak and Akeel were deep in conversation about the next stage of the paper as the takeaway worker switched some tapes on his stereo system. He turned up the sound of some Islamic Nasheeds and then turned down the volume slightly before turning it up again.

Kal got up and returned with an ashtray and promptly lit a cigarette as Zak moved his hand across the front of his face to waft away the smoke. I took a cigarette from the box and placed it behind my ear.

Akeel was dressed in his trademark ripped jeans whilst Zak today was wearing a pair of brown leather gloves to complement a tweed waistcoat.

I scanned across the menu again despite already having ordered the food. "Looks good that chicken, dunt it?" I said as I removed my jacket and placed it on the spare seat to the right of me.

"What?" asked Akeel.

"Looks good that chicken, dunt it…"

"What the fuck is a dunt?" said a confused Akeel.

I had never been asked that question before. "Well, it is dunt it."

"It's just talk, Akeel," chuckled Zak. "It's his accent."

"What does it mean?"

"It is short for doesn't it… which is short for does it not," explained Zak.

"Oh." Akeel still looked confused. "Never heard that before."

"It is more Yorkshire than Lancashire," added Zak.

I smirked. "Aye, I suppose it is."

Two young men wearing long Arab-style clothes entered and sat themselves on the next table and seemed to be conversing about their job prospects for the coming year. A white man entered and ordered some food and immediately the two men seated next to us began to speak in Gujarati. It was not common to see this and most of the time it was not noticeable, but today was different.

Zak glanced across at the two men and then at me. "See, I bloody hate it when people do that."

"Do what?" asked Akeel.

"That!" exclaimed Zak, fiddling with his phone.

I wasn't entirely sure what he meant but Akeel had noticed a real change in Zak's expression. "What?"

Zak was now staring at the two men sat at the next table.

"Why can't they just speak English?"

The two men continued to speak in their native language as the white man waited for his food. He was scanning through the menu as we sat there silently digesting what Zak had actually said. Strangely enough, no one wanted to get into a discussion just yet.

The customer's food was placed in a small cardboard box for him and he made his way out of the takeaway. The two men sat to our left reverted to speaking in a mix of English and Gujarati.

"Bullshit, that is," said Zak who was clearly in some discomfort.

"What's bullshit?" I asked.

"That there is bullshit."

"Oh dasde... (tell us)," said Kal.

It was probably better if he had not pressed him. "It is just rude, that's all. If you can speak English then carry on speaking English – why must we revert to another language when someone else enters the room?"

"Aaah, it's no big deal, Zak," revealed Akeel. "We do it too."

"Doesn't make it right, does it?" responded Zak.

The food was placed in front of us and Kal immediately ripped open the tray, throwing several fries on the floor. He picked a few up, whispered something and put them back in his tray, eating one first.

"I do it too," I admitted. "It is just a natural reaction sometimes. I don't even know I am doing it."

Zak stared at me. "I would have expected more of you. How would you like it if someone started speaking in their own language when you walked into the room?"

"As long as he doesn't call me a twat then what's the harm?" I started wolfing my food down.

Zak was not happy and continued to stare at the next table. "Yeah, but what if he *was* calling you a twat?"

"Then I would be none the wiser. I think you have a valid point, Zak, but fuck 'em. Nobody gonna stop me calling them a penchod."

Akeel laughed and then realised it might not be a joke he should have found so funny. "That's a bit shit. The thing is we don't really do it that much and we hardly swear at anyone."

Zak began to slowly pick at his food. "I don't do it. It just makes the other person uncomfortable and gives off a bad impression all round."

"Oh, it's fine," reiterated Akeel. "Do you think all those folk who go on holiday to Spain ever bother to learn the language? They expect the world to speak English and then moan that someone is speaking a foreign language here."

Kal, who had until then been busy eating, added, "There is a time and a place for everything. But I think we just do it to get a good deal."

He opened a cola can, spilling some of the contents onto the table and then took several gulps.

"It's like when," he paused and thumped his chest hoping it would help with his digestion, "we get to the counter we would get told by our mums that the price was a little too much and she would immediately know when it was time to leave the store but didn't want to make out the price was too high or offend the shopkeeper. That's where we get it from."

Zak was not convinced. "That's different. Mums can't speak English; we can. Just speak English. What's the big problem?"

The two men at the other table got up, paid for their meal and made some comments in Gujarati as they passed and left the takeaway.

"See. Just fucking rude, that is," observed Zak. "They are probably talking about us."

"Come on, Zak," said Akeel. "Even if they were, which they weren't, who gives a shit? Like Shuiaby said, as long they didn't call you a miserable bastard on the way out it does not matter."

Zak, arms folded still, had a quite frustrated expression on his face as if suggesting that we had not taken his observations seriously enough.

The takeaway owner shouted across to us, "Oh Khaana teek hai (Was the food okay)?"

"Yes, all good," shouted back Zak. "Thank you very much for asking. It's been a pleasure."

He stared back at us.

"What?" said Zak. "He understood what I said, didn't he?"

29 A FRIEND IN NEED

There is a saviour attitude to most people. We like to help anyone in need as much as we can as it makes us feel better about ourselves. Other times you want to assist someone but then realise your help is never going to be enough.

Late one Saturday night Jay walked into our offices. How he managed to track us down was beyond me. We were not exactly on any road to anywhere and getting here was at least a half hour walk from our neighbourhood.

Jay was an intelligent fellow and one who had always had a great deal of potential about him. It was eight in the evening and he was wearing a jumper and jeans and clutching a carrier bag. With the temperature as it was, I was amazed he wasn't shivering at all.

Kal looked over from his desk. "Hey, long time no see and how did you manage to find us?"

"I have my ways," replied Jay with a smile on his face. He spotted the tea station in the corner and began to help himself to the biscuits. "Do you mind if I make myself a cup of tea?"

"Why don't you sit down and I will make it." I got up from the computer and began to boil the kettle.

I could sense something was not quite right, but I decided to play dumb. We had known Jay since we were kids and he was very likeable fellow. No one had a bad word to say about him and he had always been a joy to be around, never bothering anyone with any demands.

He was a couple of years younger than us and still hung around the same crowd. "Remember that time Jav let off a stink bomb in mosque?" he said.

Always trying to outdo each other, mosque pranks had been one of the things we had been good at. Jav, another friend of ours, had smuggled in a stink bomb and let it off at 6.55pm, knowing class would be dismissed at seven. The revolting smell led to three kids being sick and the whole class area being evacuated five minutes ahead of time.

The next day, an inquisition led to everyone being punished. We couldn't possibly rat Jav out because he had, after all, pulled off the prank of the century. The memory of people running from the mosque was brought up almost every time we met any of our childhood friends.

I gazed over at Kal, "Yeah, that was a good one."

I brought Jay a cup of tea and sat down next to him. "So, what brings you here? You walked it here or did you get a lift?"

"I walked it, wasn't far." He began drinking his tea and leant back into his chair before reaching into his carrier bag.

"Listen, lads, could I interest you this?" He pulled out two packs of duvet covers, each still in their packs. "They are worth at least forty quid. I can let you have them for half price."

He handed me the sheets and I placed them on the table in front of Kal. Kal picked them up. "Where you get these? And what are you doing here at this time trying to sell us duvet covers?"

Jay was not looking like himself. I hadn't seen him for a while but today he looked a lot different to what I remembered.

Kal clearly knew what was up and as was his nature decided to be upfront. "What you on, Jay?"

Jay laughed out loud. "What do you mean? I'm not on anything."

Kal was not convinced. "It is fucking freezing outside, you have no jacket on and you just walked two miles to see us with a couple of duvets."

Jay sank back into the chair again. The boyish humour had gone.

"I'm err. Just need to know if you want to buy these covers."

Kal did not answer and neither did I.

"Okay, forget the duvets. I was thinking could you lend me £20."

Just two days earlier he had knocked at my house and I had given him £20. It was £20 I did not really have at the time, but he seemed desperate, saying he had broken something of value at home and his dad was going to kill him.

I guess I knew he was lying but I would give him the benefit of the doubt.

I stood up and walked over to get myself a biscuit. I had tended to leave any decisions to Kal. It was a complete cop out and kept me from coming across as the bad guy.

Kal placed his hands under his chin again. "I will give you the twenty quid if you tell me what you need it for? Just be honest."

Jay was someone we had known since we were kids and we did pity him.

"I just need something. That's all. Are you going to help or not?"

"No," said Kal.

"Hey why are you being a dick, Kal?"

"I said 'no', didn't I?"

"He needs our help, Kal," I interjected.

"You give him twenty quid then?" Kal turned to me. "I know what you need it for. I'm not stupid…" Jay turned away. "Show us your face."

Jay was now sat arms folded on the chair. "Don't listen to him. I just need to give the dosh to someone, that's all. It's no big deal."

It was distressing to see a friend like this but Kal was right. We were just going to be another couple of guys he had met who had would help him today.

"Shuaiby, tell him," said a frustrated Jay.

"Tell him what? You took £20 the other day. What happened to that?"

"Okay, you are right. But we are friends. What kind of friends are you two? Stop taking the piss. Are you going to help me or not?"

I sat back down opposite Jay this time. It was not easy seeing someone in such a state. "Why don't we drop you off home?"

"I don't want to go home. You could drop me somewhere else if you want."

Jay got up and began to walk around the room, whilst Kal kept a close eye on him. "Where's the toilet? This way?" and gestured towards the corridor.

I nodded and Jay hurried out of the room.

Kal glanced at me. "Follow him."

"What?" I said. "Why should I follow him? What's he going to nick? Toilet rolls?"

Minutes later Jay returned and sat back down. "So, who's lending me that money?"

"No-one," said Kal.

I reached for my pocket and searched my wallet. I only had £10 there and was contemplating giving him the money.

Kal looked at me again. "Are you stupid? We have to stop this. Best thing we can do for you is we get you some help."

"I don't need you to tell me what to do. Just today I need the money and I will start fresh tomorrow. I say Allah de Kasam I will."

Swearing on god's name was common but to do so for this was a little extreme even by my standards.

People think it is easy to deal with addiction. It happens to someone else and that person is to blame for their own addiction. If they want to really stop they will do it themselves.

It is not exactly like that at all.

I walked over to Jay and sat down next to him. Kal was right but I didn't want to really admit it. We couldn't give him some more money, it just wouldn't be fair.

"How'd you get here, Jay?"

He looked away almost ashamed of himself. "I just need…"

He sat there with tears in his eyes before realising he couldn't show such weakness in front of his childhood friends.

He paused, composed himself and gazed around the room. "You guys have got one shit office. Has nobody told you it's a fucking toilet paper factory, not a newspaper office?"

It seemed the best way out of any of us continuing an uncomfortable conversation.

I smiled and so did Kal. "Yeah, we figured it would be a good place to start a newspaper."

Jay sank back into his chair. "You guys are more stupid than you look."

30 CHAPATI

Getting a good story was getting easier. Plenty of people had now heard of the new publication and wanted to be part of it. The problem was one which many a newsroom must contend with. When do you know when someone is being genuinely truthful or is lying to get some publicity? Or how do you print something without being ridiculed for doing so? It was probably a question that had perplexed many reporters and broadcasters for countless years.

The mosque, it turned out, was becoming a great place to pick up stories because it brought together people you would rarely meet elsewhere. After prayers, people would gather outside to discuss the latest developments and current affairs, and during the holy month a particular type of story was becoming more common.

I had always been mystified about how news stories were thought up. Who told who? Somebody had once advised me the pub was a great place to pick up stories. But my audience were unlikely to be seen in pubs and clubs and the ones that did pop in, didn't really want anyone to know they had been there.

I hurried into the office a little later in the evening than normal as I had been preoccupied with a gentleman I had met through another acquaintance from my mosque.

"Okay, boys, I just met this man who says he found Allah written on a chapati and wants to put it in the paper."

Zak, Kal and Akeel all looked up at me in a state of bewilderment. Zak was the first to speak. "Oh my god."

Followed by Kal, "Oh dear. Where did you meet him? Where is he?"

I had actually brought him with me. "He's here. I thought it best we all marvel at the miracle."

Kal stood up from this chair. "Stop taking the piss."

Before anyone had a chance to react, I left the office and returned accompanied by a man with a long raincoat and shalwar kameez. It was cold outside, but I always found it strange that people still managed to wear thin shalwars (loose Asian-style pants) and slippers. He was shivering having had to wait in the car park.

He cautiously entered the room and stood in the middle. It was very much like a man meeting a group of biologists having discovered a new cure for some common disease but wasn't sure it would work. "Asalamulaikum, brothers. Thank you for seeing me."

Zak was courteous as ever. "Walaikumuslaam. How can we help?"

I gestured over to him. "Show them the rotee (chapati)."

Mr M removed the chapati delicately from a small carrier bag. He had it wrapped up in another carrier bag.

I stood over close to him. "Be careful not to drop it. Could get gunah (sin)."

Kal stared at me with a troubled look on his face. I could sense he was a little concerned I had brought this stranger to the office.

Mr M held out the chapati. "My wife was cooking and she made me this. I was just about to eat it and I saw this writing."

He held the chapati delicately in the palm of his hands. The chapati had the word 'Allah' inscribed in Arabic across the middle.

"Oh yes," Zak said. "It is there alright."

"There you can see it," I added.

Now, there was a huge difference between Kal, and Zak and me. Whilst Zak and I were willing to give people the benefit of the doubt, Kal wasn't.

"Are you guys serious?" Kal looked up at Mr M who looked a little bemused but smiled nervously.

Akeel came across the room and peered at the chapati. "Oh pai (brother) wow ."

I didn't want to embarrass the poor man and tried to appease him a little. "There, you can clearly see it."

Akeel meanwhile said what was on everyone's mind. "I'm not saying I can't see it, but it isn't really a natural phenomenon. How is that natural?"

Mr M looked over at me again.

"What salan (curry) were you about to have with it?" interrupted Zak.

I turned to Zak. "Does that matter?"

"I am just curious."

Mr M was happy to share this pointless information. "It was saag ghosht."

"Nice, "said Zak. "If you are going to dip a rotee like that into anything you can't get better than saag ghosht. You know you shouldn't have lassi with Saag, it can cause you real issues."

Kal walked away and sat down, nodding his head as if a silent protest might help people come to their senses.

"So, what do you think, lads?" I looked around the room.

Zak was as comforting as ever. "Yeah, I think it's a good story."

Akeel had warmed to the idea a little. "Have you got something a little more natural like an aubergine? Or maybe a tomato?"

Mr M stared at Akeel and then looked back at me again.

"No, he hasn't. He has got a rotee and it has clearly got Allah written on it." I turned to Mr M and nodded as if to tell him I had his back. "I have already taken a picture and got your details. So, what are you going to do with it?"

Mr M was still proud of his chapati and placed it carefully back in his carrier bag. "I am keeping it for now to show people. We have already had all our relatives come round to see it. But I think we will have to eat it later."

"Good luck with that and let us know how it goes."

"What do you mean?" asked Mr M.

"You know, if it all goes down well. You know, when you eat it." I said nodding my head.

Akeel was one of those people who couldn't hide his emotions well from people and smiled at me.

I realised it was time that Mr M left before someone said something derogatory. "Okay, thanks for coming down; I just needed to make sure the others could witness this miracle. I will see you soon."

Mr M turned to me once more. "So, will it be in the paper?"

It was tough letting people down but at this stage I couldn't go back on my word. "We will discuss it and if we can't get it in this month, we will look at it next month."

Mr M left the office. I stood at the door to check if had exited the building completely.

Akeel looked over at me. "Come on, Shuiaby. What was that?"

"It was a man with an 'Allah rotee'. It was there, you all saw it."

Akeel was still not convinced. "You could see he wrote it on there and cooked it. How is a chapati natural? His wife probably wrote it on there to get him out of the house."

"Could be natural." I sat down, placing my feet back on the desk. "Could be a miracle. Who's to know. What if it wasn't written on? What if all you fucks are wrong?"

Zak laughed. "I'm with Shuaiby. Make a great front page. I can see the headline now… HOLY ROTEE! He's only gone and dipped it in Saag Ghosht."

But it was getting tougher keeping up the pretence. "Look, I know it was bullshit, but people just like to be made to feel they are something special. You just have to be polite, that's all."

"No we don't," said Kal.

"Yes, we do. The guy clearly has some issues but to him this little thing was important. Plus, I really didn't know how to say 'no' to the guy. He was just so nice. Did you see how he was holding the rotee? And those chappals (slippers). Who wears chappals when it's minus two outside?"

"These people need hope," remarked Zak.

"These people need help," replied Kal.

It was one thing telling anyone they were a fraud but another thing doing it to their face. "We can't be rude to anyone even if he turns out to be a little eccentric."

Akeel put his hands on his head and leaned back into chair. "He wasn't eccentric. The guy needs to be told to stop bullshitting. There was no miracle there."

It was time to make the team feel guilty. "Okay, okay. I get it. But next time can we just learn to be a little polite to people who might not seem they are all there? No matter what, we have to be a little professional. That is one quality we could all do with right now."

Everyone acknowledged my plea for some diplomacy except Akeel. "Miracle my arse."

31 THE USUAL SUSPECTS

The first time you attend an event to report on a story, you quickly realise something. Some people treat you better than others. Zak had an idea about the 'type' of publication we should envisage to be. "We want to be like the Mirror – not the Times. As more people read the Mirror," he said as we parked up outside the factory.

It was all very well for him to compare our lowly free newspaper with national brands, but that was always Zak's way. The more he talked something up, the more he thought people would aspire to that level. It wasn't always the best way to go about things, especially when he was dealing with a man like myself who thought quite the opposite.

"And we can't go with a negative front page. It needs to be positive as we are supporting the community not dissing them," I added.

"We could just do what other papers do," pointed out Zak. "They put a couple of positive stories in to balance out the semi-racist features they include about minorities. That way no one can call them racist."

"And no usual suspects," I added.

"Who?" asked Kal

"You know the guys who always get in the paper because they are the only Asians the reporter knows. Anything happens and they roll out the same old faces to comment on everything from Kashmir to potholes. I mean, how is someone meant to know about the complexities of geo-politics and why the grass wasn't being cut at Saint Barnabas?"

"Some of them could be of use," said Kal.

"Like Councillor Faisel, you mean. I had the pleasure of meeting him again today."

Most newspapers had dedicated photographers but as we did not have a budget for this, it was decided one of us should take this role.

I had made myself official photographer quite quickly as it was a job that required little thinking on my part. I was wrong.

Earlier in the evening I had been attending a small charity event and been accosted by a councillor who was always in the local daily newspaper. Whenever and wherever there was an event, this man would find himself on the front row of the group picture. I had always flicked through the pages and seen this man unashamedly posing at almost every function.

It had become a long running joke but I had never actually figured out how he did it. Today, I had seen first-hand the lengths he would go to, to make the news and he was very good at it. It was very much an art form.

I had been taking the customary pictures at the function and just before the group shot he would subtly move into the frame. I have to say it was a clever way of getting oneself into the picture without the others in the group knowing he was there. Within seconds of the picture having been taken he would step out of the frame. The others were none the wiser.

When the picture was developed it was far too late to do anything about it. The whole act took place in the blink of an eye and twice now he had managed to sneak into a group picture without me knowing it.

Another time he blatantly asked me to take a picture of him even though he had nothing to do with the function at the time, because him being there was enough for him to be included in the story. This need for attention was something I hated. But he lived for this adulation. Or false adulation on his part.

"There is nothing wrong with Councillor Faisel," said Kal. "He is a lovely chap. He just likes to be in the picture, that's all. It is a Pakistani thing."

"What's Pakistani about it?" asked Zak as we headed into the factory.

"You know." Kal was finding it difficult to back up his comment with some sort of evidence. "It just is. People like to pretend they are of some importance and there is no better way to prove that to others than get yourself in the picture. We want to be seen."

"Oh, he is good at it though," I said, switching on the kettle for what seemed like the hundredth time in less than a month. "You should have seen how excited he was when I pointed the camera just at him."

Kal looked at me and smiled. "Oh yeah…"

Zak sat down at the computer. "You know why they do this? Newspapers. Always use the same person to comment on different issues?"

"They do it because it is easy. When you are up against a deadline you just ring the same fellow to guarantee a comment of some sort. With us Asians the reporter can't be bothered doing any proper research and decides to call the first brown person he or she knows."

I sat back on the leather chair. "It's different for us though, isn't it?" Both Zak and Kal looked at me. "You see, we aren't like other people, are we. We Punjabis can tell someone to fuck off."

Zak chuckled to himself whilst Kal nodded his head again in agreement. "Basically, what you are saying is that white folk are polite whilst we are a bunch of animals."

"No, it is just if we don't like anyone we kind of let them know there and then. Well, you do anyway. Myself and Zak here are far too polite to let them know our true feelings," I said.

Zak spent the next few minutes waiting for the computer to turn on. "You went to see that 'community leader' – what happened? Did they give you an advert or any good advice?"

"Not really," answered Kal. "We got some custard creams and tea and we talked about what a great guy he was. Look, I have a great amount of respect for them but most of them are just there because no one else wants to do the dirty job."

Zak finally managed to log in on the computer after several minutes of punching the enter button. "Fine, no usual suspects in the paper."

"And I am banning the words 'Community leader'," I added. "Why do we need a community leader? We call them as they are, Councillors, Moulvis and whatever else."

Kal nodded. "Yes that makes sense."

I picked up the page plan. "What's going here?

Without even looking at the sheet, Zak said, "Jack Straw."

Kal got up from his seat and took the plan from my hand. "The great dependable Jack Straw. Always looking out for the brothers."

I looked at Kal and then down at Zak. "What did we just discuss? We said NO usual suspects."

"Jack isn't a usual suspect. He's more of an unusual suspect. You can't quite tell if he is just being nice to you because he has to, or he genuinely likes you. Anyway, he is a local celebrity," said Zak.

I had realised some battles would not be won today.

I pointed to another section. "And here?"

"This is a hard news page."

"What about the story I wrote? About that charity do?"

"You mean the one with Councillor Faisel in it?"

"Yeah, that's the one. It has to go in."

Zak looked up at me. "Hold on, one minute you are saying you don't want the usual suspects in the paper and the next you want to give pride and place to the photo whore?"

Even I was a little shocked with Zak's description. "I hear what you are saying but I can't disappoint him now."

The door opened and Mohammed entered the room with a carrier bag. Mo as he was known was our childhood friend who had gone on to become a leading lawyer in the region and recently been accepted at one of the largest and most prestigious firms in the country. He was impeccably dressed as always with a long black overcoat and unlike some others seemed genuinely happy to see us. He had kindly agreed to pen a column for us entitled 'No Holds Barred', which he wanted to type himself.

I welcomed him to the office, standing up and bowing jokingly. "Mr Mohammed Saab LLB CANTAB, glad your honour could join us." I liked to mention his credentials whenever I could and he hated it.

"Piss off. How's the paper doing?"

"Okay-ish. We were just talking about Councillor Faisel."

"What about him?"

"Oh, Zak here was saying we don't need his 'type' in the paper," I said.

Zak stared at me.

"Why? You should him have in the paper. He has probably faced more barriers and problems than all of us put together." Mo looked around for a reaction but didn't get any. "What you have to understand is these guys might look like they are past their sell-by date to us, but imagine having to live through the sixties and seventies and build a new life here in the UK. The amount of racism they would have suffered would have been incomparable to what we go through.

"That is not to say we follow their lead in every which way possible, but you have to respect their efforts no matter how meagre you might think they are now."

It was typical of Mo, I suppose he liked to tell us about things we didn't really want to hear, even if it meant him coming across a lot more serious than he actually was.

Kal had his hands placed under his chin again and I was waiting for him to say something profound. He didn't.

"And another thing you must remember, we always like to think what we are going through in the present time is the worst it has ever been. It is easy to do that as we really have no idea what anyone actually went through because theirs was the silent suffering."

Even before he decided to stand up in front of a judge and jury and argue his points across, Mo had always managed to bring a sense of clarity to some of our disagreements.

"Finally, you do know some of them couldn't read or write when they got here. Imagine that for a moment."

I stood up again. "Okay, you made your point, Mo. Don't need to need to go on about it. We all know you like the sound of your own voice."

Mo laughed and made his way to the tea station in the corner. "Who's for tea? I bought some cherry cake."

I really wanted for Kal to interject and thankfully he did. "Put the Councillor picture in. He has probably told the whole of Blackburn that he is going to be in Asian Image anyway."

Zak nodded.

32 THE LAST BIT

There comes a point when you start to doubt you will ever finish something.

This was that day. We had stayed at the office late in the evening again and spent most of the time trying to figure out how to fill the pages.

All five of us were sat around the dusty room that seemed to latch on to your clothes. With only one computer everyone took turns to type their pieces.

I was sat on the computer with Imran alongside me.

I typed a headline on a page: MAN HAS HABIT OF SNIFFING FINGER AFTER STICKING IT IN HIS BELLY BUTTON.

Imran looked across to me and shook his head and then turned to the others. "Somebody take this guy off the screen; he needs a break."

Zak walked over to have a look at the screen. He was not amused. Akeel peered across from his desk and laughed out loud. "Who does that?"

"You would be surprised," I said.

I was getting bored of this and we had a week to the deadline.

"We have to write something that gets people talking. Like a column," I said. "You know, something to take the piss. When I pick a paper up, I want to read something interesting."

Kal looked up from his papers. "Yeah, he's right. Something we can call our own."

"Something to really rile people up," said Imran.

"I have been thinking," I said. "Okay let me do the first one and then anyone can write the rest. Let me see. Moulvis who eat and then pick at their food from the beards? Asian men who have a tipple and then pretend to be all religious. Juthee (slipper) chors (thieves) – people who steal shoes from mosque. That happened to Kal, that was so funny."

Kal had a blank look on his face as if I had inadvertently brought up a horrible childhood memory. "It was really cold and I came to mosque with some really cool moon boots for the snow. They were the best thing ever. Cushioned from the inside and out. The kind of boots you didn't even need socks for. Then some son of a bitch stole them."

I didn't wait for him to finish his little story. "Yeah and then the poor twat had to walk home in the mosque chappals (slippers). You know the ones that everyone must use before going for the ghusal (washing oneself). They are mosque tatee (shit) chappals."

Zak seemed intrigued. "Who did it?"

"After a thorough investigation which entailed the Moulvi checking everyone's shoes – as if the thief was going to wear them back to the mosque the next day – we never did figure out who stole them."

But there was more to the tale as Kal himself explained: "Yeah, I loved those moon boots. And do you know what the worst bit was? As I stepped out of the mosque in those 'tatee' chappals – which by the way had stains on them – it started fucking snowing."

Everyone laughed.

The festival of Eid ended Ramadan and there were a few things that we could all expect. "How about ten things I hate about Eid?" I said.

"You can't hate Eid. Moulvis will kill you," pointed out Akeel.

He was right. Religion was off limits, but the habits that we had were not.

"Come on, it will be fun."

Zak looked across from his seat. "We can't take the piss out of religion. It is suicide."

"We aren't taking the piss out of religion," I said. "Just sharing some stuff that happens on a religious day."

Imran realised that we were on to something. "Why can't we go after the Moulvis?"

I puffed out my cheeks again. "Okay, let me do it once and if it is shit we won't do it next month.

"The Eid hug, the Eid food, the money, the women dressed up as Christmas trees. My sisters got an Eid outfit once – looked like Luton Town's home kit. The guys with sweaty hands who shake your hands."

Kal stood up and paced around the room. "Okay okay, that might work. And how people race around the streets like dickheads."

"What about Eid day? We can never decide when that is?" I said.

"That's too predictable. Everyone talks about that all the time," added Imran.

Having decided that I would be the first person to write the column, we had more pressing issues. "What are we going to call it?" Kal asked.

There was silence in the room again.

And then what can only be described as a moment of genius Zak said, "How about the Last Bit: A column dedicated to the minor irritations of life."

Kal laughed. "As in the Last Bit – your last bit?"

"Yeah why not. Who's going to know?" said Zak.

I glanced over at Zak with a surprised look on my face. "The Last Bit as in THE last bit. YOUR Last Bit?"

"Indeed. The Last Bit. The greatest column ever written by any human being."

Myself, Kal and Imran repeated 'The Last Bit' in turns with Akeel exaggerating the 'THE'.

Zak nodded his head. "Okay can not everyone say it. It's done. It's named. Design it."

We sat back contemplating how this would pan out and following one bright idea came another. "Why don't have a page where people send their problems in?" said Kal.

Of course I had been speaking about this very idea earlier to my 'book girl' but hadn't had the nerve to say anything. I probably thought the guys would laugh at the suggestion, but now Kal had said it the whole thing seemed a lot more plausible.

"Like an agony aunt page?" Trying to sound completely original.

Kal was not surprised that we were both on the same wavelength again. "Yes, but for Asian problems."

Asian problems to us were a little different to 'other problems'. Of course, we were all going through the same issues in life, but 'Asian problems' were unique. It was exclusive to us from the things we ate and how we tried to balance culture and religious obligations with our daily lives.

I did think that Zak might be a little apprehensive going down this route, but he was more than happy for us to explore this. "Like visa issues," he said.

Kal had that familiar pose again, placing his hands under his chin. "No, nothing like that."

It was Akeel who thankfully dragged the paper into new territory. "Wife problems."

"Yes… and then… I mean what kind of wife problems? No, home problems in their lives. You know, like interfering family members and friends who are always getting you in trouble."

I tried once more to contribute to the debate. "Like an Asian agony aunt."

Kal glanced across to me and then back to Akeel. "It has to be problems people can really relate to."

Zak was still trying to figure out where we were going with this. "Like thinking of Arsenal when Barbara Windsor came on TV?"

We all looked at him as he chuckled to himself.

Akeel was fast becoming the only man talking any sense. "Or

going to someone's house and finding they don't have a lota."

A lota is a utensil used to wash yourself after you have been to the bathroom and truly was an 'Asian' problem if there ever was one.

Kal stood up from his seat. "No, you guys are not getting it. Like a Massi type woman who people will trust."

I tried once again to add my threepence to the latest brainstorming session. "You mean like an Asian agony aunt."

I had finally managed to win over Kal. "Yes, an Asian agony aunt but with real attitude."

"It could be done," replied Zak. "But we can't go down that route at the moment."

I guess I knew this was too good to be true and if I was going to be honest I hated it when anyone managed to find a fault with something that had potential.

"Why not?" I said.

"She can't just appear just like that – we have to ask the readers to submit their problems," pointed out Zak.

He was right, or was he?

"But the letters are all made up, aren't they?" said Kal. "No one sits there and posts a letter to an agony aunt, do they?"

Akeel laughed and put his head in his hands. "Someone must."

"We can try it but not in the first issue," said Zak. "It would be far too obvious."

I am not entirely sure what he meant by that, but it probably made sense.

"We can name it Dear Noreen or something like that. It sounds like a name you can trust. You know, I was speaking to Noreen and she told me I should leave him because he has long hair and an earring," said Kal.

There was a pause.

"All for Dear Noreen?" Zak raised his hand and we all followed suit.

"Okay wait," said Kal. "But we need to find a woman."

There was a silence again and Zak went back to his phone and then to his Filofax.

I raised my hand again this time mimicking a child wanting to answer a question in class. "I think I know just the person."

33 BOOK GIRL AGAIN

I decided to take a stroll back to the store where I had met the person I was now referring to as 'book girl'.

She was sat on her stool, hunched over a book. She spotted me come in, but I pretended that I needed to buy something so headed to the stationery section and picked up a pencil.

It was one of those stores that sold almost everything and anything, but not as run down as the others that I had frequented in the past. If I was going to be honest, she looked quite out of place here.

It was busier than normal, and a few customers browsed and then picked up what they needed and left. I walked over to the counter.

"Hi."

"Hello."

"How are things here?"

She continued to read what I could make out was '*Crooked House*' by Agatha Christie. She had switched to detective novels.

"You haven't come to sell me an advert again, have you? I don't think your first effort went too well."

"Oh no. Not at all. I was in the area and thought I would pop in and have a quick chat."

This of course was a lie. I had only come here for her.

She looked over at me again. "What do you want to talk about?"

"I have a proposition for you?"

She pulled the book away from her face and said, "Yes, yes this was sooo unexpected. Let's do it. Shall I call my parents now? They will be overjoyed."

"Oh no, not that sort of proposition." Then I realised she was being sarcastic again. "Oh, you were joking. Ha ha. Very funny indeed."

She put the marker in her book carefully and placed the book on the counter.

"What do you want then. I have a very busy schedule as you can see."

I looked around at the empty store.

"You know what. You are really funny. That was good."

She smiled. "I shall count myself as a fortunate member of the inferior sex for gaining your affections in this way."

I raised my eyebrows and nodded as if not entirely sure what that whole sentence meant.

This was not going the way I had envisaged so I decided to be completely honest with her.

"Okay, look here we are, as you know launching a newspaper and we want to have a page for problems. You know like the one you mentioned last time. And I was thinking…"

She glanced back at her book before gazing back up at me.

"Would you like to be our Massi?"

Her expression changed. "Now there are seven words I never

thought I would ever hear in my life."

I laughed. She was actually, funny, warm and engaging when you got past the somewhat defensive exterior.

"What do I have to do?" She seemed genuinely interested.

"We need you to answer the questions to problems sent in by readers."

She looked at me and scanned my face and pretended to squint.

"Seriously. You want me to be the agony aunt?"

"Yes, why not? You seem like someone we can trust with the problems of the world. All you have to do is answer them."

I seemed to have got her undivided attention at last. "Is that ALL. Answer them?"

"Yes, it was your idea in the first place so why don't you just try it out for a few months and see how it goes." I paused. "There is no money at this stage. We can't afford it yet."

She smiled again. "Why do people always have to think about money? I hate talking about money."

Okay, this was going well. She was interested and she didn't want paying either, which is important when you don't have any money to give anyone.

"Do you know something? You have a very broad Lancashire accent."

It was the not the first time someone had noticed my accent.

I wanted to sound intelligent, but I don't think I pulled it off. "Yes, well. I didn't think I did until I heard you speak."

Hearing someone ridicule your accent can be offensive and

endearing at the same time.

"You guys say 'really' a lot don't you. Every other person I meet says… 'Oh really' or should I say 'Oh raylleh'."

"Oh wait, the best one is 'Don't know Raylleh' and 'I don't know you know'."

Maybe she had a point. "Do we? It hadn't occurred to me actually."

"Oh my god you said 'Actualleh'." She sniggered.

"And what is the deal with don't worreh?" She laughed out loud at her own impression of a broad Northern accent in a deep voice. "Don't worreh, love, we can go out laytah." And laughed again.

"Okay, I must stop you there." As if I could stop her in mid-flow.

"Oh, that is so funny. Or should I say Funneh!" She laughed out loud again and this time snorted.

"Oh, you made me do the soor (pig) noise."

I attempted to change the subject by complimenting a chocolate bar of all things. "This new blue packaging is great, isn't it?"

She laughed out loud again. "Did you just say ba-loo?"

"Blue," I repeated.

"You said Ba-lu. Say slow."

"No, I'm not saying it. Okay fine. Slow."

"Oh my god you said sa-low."

She shook her head, smiled and realised she had strayed from our initial discussion. I was almost glad I had amused her in this way.

"Okay, back to what we were talking about. Me being your agony aunt. Yes, I could give it go but we have to have a few rules."

I hope she keeps them simple. I had no real idea what publishing rules and etiquettes were. Were there any?

"Number 1, I need to remain anonymous. No one must know I am Massi jee (Auntie). If at any time I think that my identity is being compromised, then the deal is off."

I nodded again. This wasn't exactly the secret service.

"Number 2: We are NOT going to go down the crude route unless there is a genuine reason. If the letter asks about 'you know what' then we leave it unless there is a genuine reason for it to be tackled. As you have to consider the attitudes and perceptions of the people reading this."

I nodded again. "Yes, makes sense."

"And number 3: This has to be a safe place for people to talk about things going on in every household. So, just because you blokes don't like it, doesn't mean it doesn't happen."

I didn't understand the third point.

"Agreed. To all three."

At that very moment the door opened and a middle-aged portly gentleman entered the store. I knew of him and had met him on occasions at the odd funeral or wedding. He was wearing a faded grey checked suit and blue slip-ons.

"Hello, how are you?" Gesturing towards Book Girl.

"I am well, uncle. The usual?"

"Yes please."

She handed over a packet of cigarettes from behind the counter.

"Well then, baytee (daughter but used to refer to a younger woman), I am very busy today. It is hard doing all this charity work for people.

You know I don't really like to take credit for things, but I like to help people. That is my motto. Just help people.

"You know my son he came home the other day and said to me, 'Dad, how come you work so hard for other people?'

"You do know my son he works for a big company. A lot of money. He drives a silver Mercedes, you know. He also eats feta cheese."

Book Girl listened attentively. "That's wonderful." I could sense she was being polite for the sake of it but she did it so well.

"Yes, yes like I was saying, he tells me that I should be getting an MBE for my efforts. You know for helping people all the time. It is not the first time anyone has said that to me.

"People say that to me all the time that I should be awarded for this.

"But you know, I am far too humble for anything like that. I would rather not tell anyone about this. You know, keep it quiet and work behind the scenes."

We both looked at each other.

He then turned to me. "And what about you? What do you do?"

I looked over at Book Girl and she back at me and then back at uncle. "I… err, well, nothing. I was just here buying things."

"Oh well, I have to go. We have a big meeting later today and I have to do a special iftari."

He glanced at us and we both looked at each other again.

I could never understand this inherent need to tell the next person that you were doing some sort of charity work. If you were doing some good deed then just do it, I had always thought. Did that not simply defeat the whole purpose of doing something good and helping out someone less fortunate? I swear, some people simply did these things to make sure they could tell the next man what a wonderful person they were. It was a quality I could never understand in anyone.

Book Girl smiled and waited for the shop door to close and said, "And number 4: I do not want to be awarded. I do not want to be credited in any way nor are you to nominate me for an MBE."

I laughed out loud.

"I met his son once and he kept telling me about how he had scratched that gleaming car. If ever I felt a sense of Schadenfreude then that was it," she added.

I frowned and nodded again in agreement to something I did not fully understand.

She turned to pick up a copy of Jane Austen's *Pride and Prejudice* and held it out in front of me.

"Do Kasam on this."

I smiled at her again. This was unusual.

"Okay, I swear on this leather-bound copy of Pride and Prejudice that I have not smelt but would very much like to, I will abide by the four rules of Massi. Never to be broken."

She placed the book back on her small shelf.

"Good."

"Good," I replied.

"Okay then."

"Okay then, I will be off and will be in touch. Whenever that may be."

She picked up her copy of Crooked House and peered back at me. "Good."

34 ONE RULE FOR ONE

Desmond's was the best thing on TV since as far back as I can remember. It was a working-class view of life in the inner cities and many Asians could relate to the pitfalls of family life.

Up until Goodness Gracious Me hit the screens, Asians were either shopkeepers or extremists. Goodness Gracious Me was different. It was the first time many of us had seen something on national television that smashed the many stereotypes we had grown up with.

Sayed worked at a factory and as we took over the office in the early evenings, he would make his way into the room to talk about his life and family.

On this particular day he looked a little more forlorn than normal and was waiting for his son to pick him up after another long shift.

Khalil and I were in the office and the radio was playing Puff Daddy's 'Missing You'.

Sayed walked over to the radio and turned it down. "Why do some of our guys need to be black? I mean black music, black clothes and black attitude."

There was a growing feeling that our culture was being eroded by our being born here and living in the UK. Sayed seemed a likeable chap when I had first met him, who was genuinely interested in what we were doing and popped in every so often to talk about cricket and politics. Today, things felt a little different.

"Uncle, there is nothing wrong with that, is there?" I said. Realising that maybe asking a question wasn't the best thing to do.

He sat down on a chair in the corner. "What is wrong with being proud Muslim men? Why must you do this to your hair and why must you wear these clothes? Look at my son. He thinks he's more black than he is Asian."

Kal sat behind the computer and waited for it to boot up. "It doesn't matter, does it? It is just style."

"We have no culture here really. What is it with black culture that makes it so attractive to us? We are not like them. We are Muslim. Look at our girls – they have started wearing jeans."

It was a common gripe some Asians would bring up in conversations and it wasn't the first time we had heard this.

Black culture had had a huge impact on our communities because it had for many years been the foremost feature on style, music and film. Yet, it was frowned upon by some who felt it had replaced our own culture.

This had in turn led to stereotypes and a deal of racism from within our own culture towards the black community. We liked to kid ourselves and hide behind the notion that we Muslims were not racist and that this type of prejudice didn't exist, but it did.

People also liked to align nationality with religion and many a time the terms were interchanged to prove a point.

Kal was his forthright self. "I don't understand people," added Kal. "One minute you say we are too white and the next too black."

Sayed got up from his seat and paced across the room and sat back down again. "Why do we need to be like either? We should be like ourselves. Be proud of our Pakistani and Muslim culture. I am not a racist and I like all people, but this black music and the way they act – my son is just every day making new hairstyles and wearing these clothes to be like them. He is turning into a bandar every day."

Sayed laughed and seemed a little surprised that we refused to join in.

Bandar, translated as monkey, was a disgusting term to describe black people.

Kal looked over at me and then back to Sayed. "Uncle, that is just plain racist what you just said."

"What?"

"That word you used."

"You mean bandar?" And laughed to himself again.

"Yes, how would you like it if someone called you a Paki?"

There was an awkward silence.

Sayed didn't like to be challenged in this way. "That is different." He stretched. "Why is this so bad?"

Unfortunately, it wasn't the first time we had heard this, but on this occasion it was coming from someone whom I had thought would be far more accepting.

"We can't have one rule for us and one rule for everyone else," I said. "We want everyone to treat us equally and then talk about other people in this way."

Sayed wasn't about to let this go so easily. "What? You want our children to forget where they came from? Our Islam? What do you want them to do?"

"No one is saying forget anything," said Kal. "You just can't use disgusting shit like that to describe people."

There was another awkward silence, broken by Sayed. "Why do they want to be black?"

"Let him be and I am sure everything will be fine," I said. "What if he meets a nice black girl and wants to get married. What will you do then?"

Sayed seemed almost offended by the suggestion. "Why, is he thinking of something?"

"Oh no, not at all, I was just saying. Times are changing and people need to be more accepting, that is all."

He glanced over at Kal who was busy typing on the computer now. "I have no issue really with marriage and people. Islam teaches us to treat all people equally. He can marry whoever he wants as long it isn't a kalee (black), goree (white), Indian or wahabbi."

Kal stopped typing. "Oh bhai you should be glad he marries a woman."

I tried my best not to laugh whilst Sayed sat there silently and frowned; thankfully he didn't fully understand what Kal had suggested.

"What does your son do now?" I said before he had time to think.

"He is a student studying Engineering."

"That is something to be proud of. Tough course, that is."

"Yes, it is."

Kal got up from his seat to make himself some tea. "Listen, Sayed Bhai. Can I give you some advice? Everything will be fine. Compared to the kind of trouble kids are getting themselves into these days, you have done a good job in raising him. Your son is clever and no matter what happens he is still your son. You should be proud. Just don't come out with that racist shit again."

Sayed seemed a little more relaxed having been told he had been a good parent.

"Also," added Kal, "like I always say, unless you are brave enough to use those words in front of the people you are offending, then don't say them at all."

Sayed nodded to himself.

"Thank you."

"For what?" I said.

"Just thank you."

35 THE YUKKA PLANT

Without a car you can't really do anything. Those who say you should walk or take the bus do not have to walk in the freezing rain to a meeting and pretend you parked your vehicle around the corner.

I had walked to the town centre on this particular day and arranged for Zak to pick me up later so we could head to the office.

Zak drove a newish Vauxhall Astra and I waited on Richmond Terrace in the town centre for him.

I got in and put my hands on to the heater and then to my mouth to warm them up. "Put the heating up, mate."

He had more pop music playing in the background and instead turned up 'Hand on your heart' by Kylie.

"What the fuck, Zak?"

He glanced across. "What?"

"Why am I sat in the car with another grown man listening to Kylie?"

"Because you were born a very lucky man."

I raised my eyebrows and turned the music down and fidgeted around for the heating dial myself.

"Who have you been to see?"

The car began to warm up. "Oh that 'importer exporter' who has a BMW and a gold watch and thinks he is some sort of modern-day Jay Gatsby. He knows one of my neighbours and wanted to meet up for a chat."

Asians and wealth went hand in hand and we really loved to flaunt our wealth. We had not made a secret of the fact that we hated this trait in people and anyone showing off their wealth was trying to distract the attention away from having no personality.

Zak glanced across to me. "So he wasn't a drug dealer then?"

I raised my eyebrows again. "You see it is comments like that which makes me question how much you actually want to support the brothers. No, he wasn't a drug dealer nor was he involved in any sort of criminality. He is just a guy who likes to buy expensive things to impress people."

I am not even sure that Zak was paying attention to me sometimes. He took a slight detour and headed back to pick up Akeel, who for some reason was standing outside his house in the cold.

Akeel got into the back of the car. "How's it going, lads?"

"Yeah, good. Just went to another meeting. Might get an advert out of this one."

"Who?" asked Akeel.

"You know Yaqs, the importer exporter."

"You mean the drug dealer," Akeel said, which led to Zak immediately chuckling to himself.

I looked back at Akeel and then across to Zak. "Come on, guys,"

I sighed. "Not every Asian guy with a flash BMW is a drug dealer, you know? Quite a lot of them just have bad taste. The problem some of us have is that we are just not good at the subtle thing. We like to attract attention to ourselves by boasting about our pennies and we can only do it by having a nice car, nice watch and marble tables in the front rooms."

Akeel interjected, "And white suits."

Zak laughed out loud.

"Okay white suits if this was 1977," I said. "Take for instance this Yaqs guy I went to see. He imports and exports some shit, but it is just such a vague job title that to the untrained eye he can pretend to be far richer than he actually is. So, when he is invited to someone's house for a marriage proposal and people ask his dad what his boy does for a living, his dad can say, 'My son is an importer exporter'.

"It is all about giving off an impression of success which unfortunately helps to perpetuate the myth amongst others that he may have made his money through illicit means – which, may I add, he hasn't.

"If he didn't have a gold tooth, a gold watch and talk about himself so much then we wouldn't need to think he was a drug dealer. Simple really."

Zak began fiddling with the CD player and turned up another track on his Kylie album. "Listen to this one, Akeel, you will love this."

Akeel was sat leant forward through the seats. "Sonia?"

Zak ignored Akeel's poor attempt to guess the artist. "What did you talk about with this Yaqs guy then?"

"We went through a few things about young people and how it was important for businesses like his to support them. And how drug dealing is causing huge issues in our community and needs to be tackled."

Zak nodded his head. "What's his office like then?"

"It was a nice set up – all the mod cons. Clearly doesn't beat a toilet paper office and it had a large plant in the corner. You can always tell someone is something if they have a nice Yukka plant. Anyway, he is going to get back to me."

Zak turned up his Kylie track as we pulled into the 'dark end of Blackburn' as I liked to call it. We headed into the office where Kal was busy on the computer, putting together some invoices.

He didn't lift his head from the screen. "So, then, lads where have you been?"

"Shuaiby went to see Yaqs… the 'importer-exporter' worker," pointed out Akeel.

"You mean the smack dealer?"

"Not you and all, Kal. Like I explained to these guys, he is valuable member of the business community who happens to have a very good Yukka plant in the corner of his office."

Kal turned from the computer screen and scratched his head. "Did you happen to ask him what he imports and exports?"

"Well, I did, but he didn't seem to want to tell me."

"That's because he imports and exports drugs, you knobhead." Both Akeel and Zak laughed.

"Oh, okay and how would you know that?"

"His name for starters, everyone knows him as Yaq the Smack. Even his dad calls him that. Did you notice there was no one else there? There is no business. It is just a front to launder money. Bet there was a car salesroom next door too?"

Obviously, I felt quite cheated by this revelation. "There may have been a car sales place next door. And come to think of it he didn't have any filing cabinets anywhere or any paperwork."

Kal laughed. "He was probably checking you out to see who you were. Thankfully now he thinks we are all just a bunch of stupid twats so has nothing to worry about."

"Yeah, okay then." I sat down on the swivel chair behind a desk.

Kal turned back to the screen and ran his hand through his hair. "Which might prove to be the best move ever. Well done, Khan."

36 WORF IS NOT A SELL OUT

"What's your favourite part of town, Zak?"

Our town had few places that you could call 'iconic' so this was not going to be easy coming up with a favourite place. Kal, Zak and I had been working late and with a week to go until the deadline, the nights were getting longer and more tedious.

"I don't know." Zak yawned and put his hands behind his head. "I would say the Spread Eagle really. It is a little out of the way."

It was probably the type of answer I had begun to expect from Zak.

"What about you, Kal? And you can't say home as that is far too obvious."

Kal got up and paced around the room and took out another cigarette and tapped it on a desk. "Hmmm, good question that. El Grecos."

El Grecos was a small restaurant based under a ramp in the town centre. As children we would pass it and look through the circular windows and peer in to see these 'rich' people tucking into their fish and chips. It wasn't until years later when we ventured in ourselves that we realised this was most likely the most common and down to earth restaurant in town.

"El Grecos. Oh nice," said Zak. "That cheese and onion pie is the best."

I looked at them both. "And?"

"And what?" asked Kal.

"Aren't you going to ask me?"

Zak shrugged his shoulders. "Well?"

"Okay, I would say the best part of town is that piss-stained subway near Church Street."

"Oh, come on," said Kal.

This subway, no longer than 100 metres, ran underneath Salford in the town centre and connected the market area with the train and bus stations. It was not a pretty place.

"I will tell you why." I stood up. "It is so us. It is a subway, stained with years if not decades of urine, connecting two places that don't need to be connected, and whenever you walk through it you never actually know if you are going to make it to the other side. I mean, who else would build something so pointless. It is a modern marvel, is it not? And most of all it smells of Blackburn."

"Fuck off," said Zak. "Weirdo."

Kal laughed but didn't bother responding to my observation.

It was getting close to midnight now and our attentions turned to the only window in the office. I got up to quickly peer through the window. "I recognise that car, lads. Just what we need."

Moments later, in walked Rizzie. "What's happening, sell-outs?"

Zak put his head in his hands and Kal looked up to the ceiling.

Rizzie was one of those guys who used the term 'sell-out' in every conversation. This could be frustrating for anyone who wasn't actually a 'sell out' – whatever that was.

"What do you mean sell outs? What we sell outs from?" said Zak.

Rizzie made his way across the desks and began to pick up pages. "This!" He pointed to a page. "This is what I meant. You are going to be another rag that bows down to their masters in the hope it will help elevate you to some new position of power."

We all looked a little frustrated as he returned to his favourite subject. Yet, we couldn't help but get into the discussion.

"It is Asians like you that get themselves into organisations and then sell the rest of us down the river. I would use the phrase Uncle Tom but that would be far too polite for you fucks."

It was becoming increasingly common for phrases like 'Uncle Tom' to be bandied about. In this case it was anyone who would aspire to serve his white masters instead of standing up for his own people.

I got up from my seat. "It has been a tiring night and we haven't got time to listen to your bollocks." I paused. "You will be calling us all coconuts soon."

Rizzie laughed. "You are coconuts."

"In fairness I am not a coconut as I am not dark enough on the outside. I am more of a peach," responded Zak.

A coconut was a term used to describe someone who was white on the inside and brown on the outside and was used in tandem with the term Uncle Tom whenever the subject of loyalty was broached.

"I don't see what the problem is," said Kal. "What's actually wrong with being a coconut? All of us are genuine coconuts now. We all want to be perceived to be in tune with our culture, but let's be honest, we are more British than Pakistani. Just because you listen to a few Nusrat Fateh Ali tracks and can rattle off a few Punjabi swearwords doesn't make you cultured, you know."

Rizzie sat back in his seat and had a habit of smiling when he had no response, but responded nonetheless. "Of course you would say that as you are a freshie."

Even I chuckled at his warped hypothesis. "I hate anyone who calls anyone a coconut," I said. "It all masks our own insecurities and we only use it to make ourselves stand out from other people."

Kal smiled. "The reason we want to label others is that it helps make us feel we are more Muslim, we are more Pakistani, we are more Indian, we are more Bengali. Think about it: most of us speak English, do everything other British people do and then when it suits us we pretend to love our culture and religion. Just be upfront about it from the beginning."

It was getting a little tedious listening to people label one another all the time. We had spent our teenage years hearing others label each other in the hope it would help to stand them apart. In the end none of it really mattered as we were all struggling to balance one part of our lives with the other.

"It is a bullshit term," I said. "If you think about it, we may not like it but we are all coconuts now. Even you?"

Rizzie looked a little surprised and offended at the same time. "Me?"

"Yes, what's the difference between you, me..." I glanced at Kal.

"And Zak here. We would be classed as coconuts and would therefore in your thinking also be 'Uncle Toms'."

Rizzie shook his head. "Oh no, you can be a coconut and not an Uncle Tom."

Kal laughed. "Like yourself."

Zak chuckled to himself. "Welcome to the club, bounty boy."

Despite our differences there was always something quite unique about Rizzie in that he would question almost every opinion anyone had. It was a remarkable trait to have in that he would also have an answer for every single point of view even if it meant upsetting people.

"Typical," replied Rizzie. "Just answer me one question. Are you going to sell us down the river?"

"What fucking river?" said Kal. "Listen to yourself, we haven't even printed anything yet. How do you know what we are going to be like? Did you just come here to abuse us?"

Rizzie chuckled to himself. I think he just enjoyed being in a place he wasn't actually welcome. I think he also revelled in just being in a crowd of people where he would heroically stand up against everyone else in the room. "I am just curious, that's all. No need to get your knickers in a twist."

There was a strange silence in the room as Rizzie helped himself to some biscuits in the corner.

"Hey, don't touch the Jaffa cakes," I shouted across. "People like you only deserve the custard creams."

Rizzie laughed and opened the packet of Jaffa Cakes, gesturing towards me as he did so.

"Can I ask you a question, Rizzie?" I said.

Rizzie proceeded to boil himself some water. "What?"

"Do you think Worf is a sell out?"

Unknown to many, Rizzie was an avid Star Trek fan. Worf was the Klingon character who served on the USS Star Ship Enterprise in the TV series The Next Generation. Rizzie sat himself down in front of me. "What's your point?"

"You see, Worf as you know is a Klingon and you may recollect that on many episodes he has to prove his loyalty to either Starfleet or his species. In one particular story he comes across renegade Klingons who are being pursued by another Klingon ship. Worf is told that he must prove his loyalty to them or to the captain of his ship."

Rizzie smiled. "And?"

"He ends up making a choice and eventually kills the Klingon who is threatening to blow up the whole ship and go down in a blaze of glory."

Kal glanced over at Rizzie. "So then is Worf a sell out and an Uncle Tom?"

Rizzie clearly didn't want to say anything against Worf. "That's different."

"Can you not see the parallels though?" I said. "If after all the shit you have been spewing for the past few weeks, Worf would be classed as a sell out and Uncle Tom."

Rizzie walked back to the fridge for some more biscuits. This time picking up the custard creams. "Worf is not a sell-out nor is he an Uncle Tom. You see, Worf works for the betterment of his people and he wants to represent his people in the best way he can. Anyway, you can't compare yourselves to Worf just because you have a slight resemblance to him." Rizzie laughed and glanced over at Kal. "Worf questions and challenges his captain all the time. They are people you and I know who have sold their souls to the betterment of themselves and not to the higher cause."

I looked over at Kal and then Zak. "The parallels are there though, aren't they? Worf is challenged over his beliefs and ideals by his Klingon brethren for simply wanting to do the right thing. He can't really win, can he, unless he becomes a 'true Klingon' or 'a model Starfleet officer'."

Kal patted Rizzie on the back and took the last biscuit from his hand. "Good Point that, Khan. This guy is more of a Ferengi anyway."

A Ferengi was a species form the same series whose whole society was based on profit and their scheming ways to manipulate others would regularly lead them to ruin.

Rizzie got up from his seat. "It doesn't change a thing, this. None of it does. This country has far too many sell outs and Uncle Toms and we don't need any more. People who will sell their souls for a pat on the back from their masters. That's why we are where we are."

I stood up. "You never know, we might even surprise you. We could well turn out like Worf."

Zak stared at us all. "I would love to discuss more sci-fi bollocks, but have you all forgotten we have a paper to print? Rizzie, can you leave please." Rizzie headed back to the fridge. "And leave the custard creams – you don't even deserve them."

37 DEADLINE

Barely a month since we sat in a takeaway talking up this 'idea', we gathered at a toilet roll factory to publish a newspaper. If I am going to be honest, I did not think this was going to happen. We had managed to raise enough money and the paper was complete. Or so we thought. A print deadline is like no other thing in the world and can break even the strongest of souls.

Every single day for the past week we had worked until 5am to ensure we could meet this blasted deadline, but now we felt a little apprehensive and worried that we may miss it completely. We got together early evening for the final push over the line.

Bamboogie by Bamboo played on the radio and Kal walked over to turn it up and began nodding his head.

No sooner had he done so Benny was back in the office for an update, shouting, "Alright fuckwits." He walked over to turn the music down. "Don't you haramees know it is still Ramadan? You should have a na'at (religious poetry) on or something."

The very notion of using a swear word to remind us of the religious holy month didn't seem to bother Benny very much.

"Come on!" exclaimed Zak. "We are busy, go away."

"I am meeting someone here."

Hearing those five words coming out of Benny's mouth left us with a sense of dread. It was not the first time he had done this, but tonight we were tired, stressed and simply did not have time to deal with this intrusion by a man who cared little about our predicament.

I put my notepad down. "Who the hell are you meeting here?"

He stood there silently in the middle of the room as if to suggest he was the man in charge and I was simply a lowly worker whom he could treat with the contempt I deserved. "In fact, wait, he might be outside."

Benny hurried away and returned minutes later with a stocky man with a small black dog. Akeel jumped up from his seat and Kal wanted to join him but pride stopped him from showing any real fear.

Asians and dogs didn't go well together where we were concerned. We had grown up largely fearing them because the only dogs in our neighbourhood tended to be guard dogs or had owners who would taunt us with the odd racial remark thrown in. I had always thought it a pity that an innocent dog could end up with an owner who was a son of a bitch.

"Okay then," I said, trying to be polite as possible. "How can we help you and your friend here?"

Benny gestured to the man to sit in a seat in the corner. "This is Baz and his dog Oliver."

There was silence in the room as we attempted to work out what was going on. Benny had seemed to have really baffled us tonight.

Kal shook his head and held his hands up. "And?"

Far from being embarrassed Baz looked relaxed and happy to be in a toilet factory surrounded by five young men he had never met. Anyone else may have been a little apprehensive but I guess this was the power of Benny – he could make anything seem strangely normal.

Benny paused for a moment to ensure he had everyone's attention. "Well, Oliver is Asian and does tricks."

Akeel and Imran both laughed out loud.

"I see your point," said Zak. "And?"

Benny always liked to give off the impression that he was the boss of almost any organisation and business. "This is an Asian paper, isn't it? Baz, show him."

Baz, a well-dressed middle-aged gentleman wearing glasses, got up from his seat and beckoned his pet to jump up on to the desk and back down again. Oliver then flipped over on himself. As he did so Akeel moved away towards the door.

Zak remained seated behind his desk, but I could sense he was pretending not to let on that he was afraid of the animal.

"He can do a lot more but it is best to do it outside," said a smiling Baz.

I glanced across at the others. "What's our deal with four-legged Asians, Kal?"

Kal got up from his seat, went over to Benny and placed his arm around him. "Good story this, Benny, and well done for bringing Baz and Oliver to our attention. Maybe we can catch up later. We are kind of busy at the moment."

Benny with his arms still folded looked up at Kal and then across at Baz. "Okay, okay, I see what is going on here. You guys are racist."

"How can we be racist?" I said.

"You don't want to do the story because Baz here isn't Asian."

"That's got nothing to do with it? It is just it is deadline night and we have ten hours to print a newspaper." I turned to Baz. "No offence, Baz, but your dog is brilliant. I love the flip thingy he just did."

Imran had remained quiet up until then. "How do we know the dog is Asian?"

Baz was about to open his mouth but was interrupted by Benny. "Oh he's Asian alright. Little bastard loves ghosht (lamb) and squats when he shits."

Akeel laughed out loud and Zak put his hands over his face.

I put my arm around Benny and walked him to the door whilst keeping a close eye on the dog. "We have seen enough. Let's talk about this next week." Then I turned to Baz. "Thank you, Baz, this was lovely, but I will get your details off Benny here. Just today is not the right time."

I returned to the office and sat down and looked across at the others. Keeping people like Benny from the office had been much harder than we had thought.

No sooner had Benny left than Zak received a text. He looked down and then stood up from his seat. "Okay that Jinn guy is coming here."

"What is this, crazy bastard night at the paper factory!" said Akeel.

I had started wondering what had happened to that story earlier. I was all for covering contentious issues, but I had quickly realised that doing so meant actually sitting and talking to people for a certain amount of time. And time was not something we had now. It was far more important to keep to a deadline so we wouldn't end up disappointing the advertisers.

"Hey, whilst we wait for this guy, Imy, tell Kal the joke about the fellow who says switch off the light."

Imran laughed. "Okay, these four friends are staying together and every night…"

"No, say it in Punjabi. It sounds shit in English."

Imran was about to open his mouth before I interrupted him again. "And do the voice."

At that point we heard a loud knocking sound on the shutters. Seconds later, a man dressed in a Shalwar kameez and winter coat entered and sat himself in front of Zak. He proceeded to tell Zak that he could in fact exorcise demons and wanted to advertise these services in the newspaper.

As always when someone new came to the 'office', it was customary for the others to remain quiet.

With deadline looming, Zak proceeded to ask the man about Jinns or demons. "I'm really sorry, but I will have to use the word 'exorcise'. So, who did you exorcise recently?"

The man who introduced himself as Usman told us of a family he had been to see recently. "We spoke on the phone and that dad I told you about. He had a John Wayne Jinn inside him. It was not good for him."

Now, such incidents were new to us but there is nothing more important than keeping a level of decorum and diplomacy when dealing with such subject matter. Well, I would like to say we were all the same, but Zak was a little forthright some days. This was one of those days.

He fiddled with his pen like he always did when he simply wanted to get out of something but didn't want anyone else to know he may well be in over his head. "Why? I mean I would be happy to have John Wayne inside me."

I glanced across at Akeel and Kal who both looked a little shocked.

Usman was not taken aback. "It was ruining his life. He couldn't sleep or eat."

Zak began to press Usman further. "I mean, did he say it was John Wayne or Marion Robert Morrison?"

"John Wayne."

"But did you ask him? Because Marion Robert Morrison is John Wayne's real name?"

"No, I never got that far really."

"So, it could have been John Wayne in disguise or someone pretending to be John Wayne really." He paused, "Forget about that. More importantly, did he get rid of him?"

"Oh yes, definitely. But I need to see him a few more times yet."

"So, you charge for this service?"

Usman remained straight faced throughout the exchange. "Yes, yes I do. But I don't ask, they just pay what they want. In Islam there is mention of Jinns. Surely you must believe that Jinns exist?"

It was a loaded question and one which Zak avoided altogether.

"Oh, so I could hire you and pay you a quid."

"Well yes but people tend to pay more than that."

"They would, wouldn't they, otherwise you wouldn't have two hundred quid to put an advert in?" asked Zak.

Usman surprisingly was not taken in by the line of questioning.

Zak continued. "So, what are we putting in the advert?"

I looked across at Zak as if to say, Are you serious? We can't run an advert from someone who says he can exorcise demons. Not now. We only have hours to publish this newspaper.

Thankfully Usman was now having second thoughts. "It is two hundred pounds, you say?"

"Yes, that should get you a decent size."

"Okay, can I let you know about this? I will have to think about it. I am not sure how many Jinns I would have to remove to pay for that?"

There was an awkward silence in the room and I pretended to stir some tea in an empty cup to look busy.

"Just another thing that was bothering me," said Zak. "If you get possessed by a celebrity do you charge more?"

Usman looked a little puzzled. "Well, it depends…" He paused.

Kal walked over the desk. "It is okay, Usman, once you decide what you want to do, maybe get back to us and we can have a chat." He then looked across at Zak.

Usman got up and shook everyone's hands and left.

I walked over to the door to check if he had gone and turned back to everyone else in the office. "What the fuck, Zak? John Wayne Jinn. We need to talk about this from now on."

Zak was not apologetic. "What's there to talk about? There is no way he was going to put an advert in. He just thought we would be so intrigued we would give it for free."

Imran was clearly a little incensed with what he had just seen. "It would have been easier not to invite the guy here. I mean, we aren't going to ridicule these people, are we?"

"He's right," I added. "We don't need to take the piss out of everyone who's a bit funny in the head."

Akeel was not convinced. "I don't think there was anything wrong with him. I think he was trying it on with us. Good one, Zak. I did not know Marion Morrison was John Wayne's real name."

"Okay, new rule," I said. "Only myself and Imran are permitted to meet those who claim to have been in touch with the nether world."

Zak chuckled to himself and Akeel laughed out loud. "Get a crazy guy to interview a crazy guy. Perfect."

Kal took a call on his mobile and walked into the other room. He came back in looking a bit disappointed.

"What's the matter, run out of toilet roll again?" I said.

"That quarter page on page seven, we will have to drop it. Son of a bitch says he doesn't want to go in anymore."

Losing an advert at this stage was bad news for us, especially when we had already missed our target. "What'd he say?" asked Akeel.

"He says he discussed it with his wife and she doesn't think it is a good idea."

Zak put his hands at the back of his head. "Now, why would he want to talk to his wife for?"

Imran tried to keep things upbeat again. "Do we know who his wife is?"

"Why would we know who his wife is?" Kal said.

"We could get one of our women to ring one of his women. You know how this shit works?"

I looked at Imran. "No, I don't know how this shit works. What, we going to get my mum to ring his mum who will ring his wife and tell him to put the advert in."

Imran frowned. "It worked for Veeru in Sholay."

The night was wearing on but somehow things were coming together much by chance than any sort of planning.

"What are we doing with this halal food story?" I held up a piece of paper.

Earlier, I had interviewed a man who says he visited a shop and was not happy with the owner not being able to prove the food was '100 per cent' halal. If there was one thing that would make people panic, it was a rumour about any store 'not being halal'. Any element of doubt could destroy the reputation of a business.

Kal walked over from his desk. "What the owner say?"

"He said he bought it from the halal butchers like everyone else."

"So, what's the problem?"

"He's not got any certification up in his shop. So, this other guy is telling everyone that it is not halal. Then secretly he told me that the guy was a Shia."

Kal chuckled to himself. "Oh, that's the shit right there. Guy's a Shia so the food must not be halal."

"Bullshit. Tell him to go fuck himself," said Akeel.

I shook my head. "Okay, I won't be doing that but will tell him we are looking into it and we will discuss this at the next editorial meeting." I scrunched the paper up and threw it in the bin.

If there is one thing about a deadline, you learn to make decisions quickly and normally they are the right ones.

It was getting late and the last thing we needed was another interruption. Zak's phone rang and he asked Akeel to answer it so he could continue on the paper.

"Hello."

For a few seconds Akeel listened to the caller.

"I see."

Slowly, his voice took on a more nervous tone.

"I understand. But…"

I glanced over. "Everything okay?"

He looked back at me and then at Kal and then at Zak waving a hand in panic.

"Well, she isn't here but I can assure you we will pass your message on."

I hastily got up and stood close to Akeel and could hear the voice of a softly spoken but stern gentleman.

"Are you able to call back in five minutes and I can pass the message on?" said Akeel and he hung up.

He sat down. "We are fucked, lads. That was the police. They want to speak to Zaika Akkas because they said there has been a complaint. Bet it was that chapati guy."

Zak continued to type as Kal got up to check the phone. "Number does not show."

I took the phone from Kal. "He is going to ring back in five minutes? Okay then I will answer it."

Right on queue the phone started bleeping and I introduced myself as Mr Khan. The male on the other side who said he was a police inspector spoke of his insistence of wanting to be put in contact with Zaika Akkas. The others stood around me and leaned over to listen to the conversation as I waved them all away.

The man continued to ask for an audience with Zaika Akkas.

"I can assure you, sir, that Ms Akkas takes all complaints seriously whatever they may be," I said, hoping he would eventually give up.

There was a pause and then things got a little serious. "You do realise that falsifying the existence of an individual to make yourselves seem more important than you really are is a criminal offence."

I frowned. Then put my hand on the mouthpiece. "How the does this guy know about Zaika Akkas? Everyone who does is in this room."

Then it dawned on me. That was untrue as I had told one other person. Akeel began to pace around the room as Imran pretended not to look so bothered. I turned my attention back to the conversation. "Mo. You are a bastard if there ever was one."

There was silence and then to my relief the sound of laughter. "I had you guys going there for a minute, didn't I?"

I puffed out my cheeks and then smiled nervously. "These guys were shitting it but I knew all along it was you." The truth is I didn't.

"Can you piss off now. This was not the time for a phone call like that."

The toughest part of publishing a newspaper is coming up with headlines. I say this because it is an art in itself and any person who thinks otherwise has not sat in front of a screen trying to find the correct amount of words to fit into a constricted space. The task is made even more difficult when you haven't slept for several days.

"I need to find a headline for this. Any ideas?" Zak rubbed his eyes and yawned again.

We all walked over to stand behind Zak. "What's it about?" asked Imran.

"It is about some bullshit snooker venue having an upgrade. Man, you couldn't find a more boring story."

I was a bit offended. "Don't knock my story, Zak."

"It *is* boring, Shuaiby," added Kal.

Everyone stood there in complete silence. It felt like climbing a mountain only to be stopped in our tracks by an extremely tricky section of the terrain. I knew something would be our undoing sooner or later. This was it.

"SNOOKER VENUE CHANGES IMAGE," said Akeel.

"Nice," said Zak. "Okay, this is about Jack Straw backing that Muslim school."

Again we stood there in silence. "Come on, lads."

"CHAUDHRY BACKS SCHOOL," I said. "Why can't we use Punjabi words with English words in the headline? It would make things so much easier."

"Because this is a newspaper. An English newspaper? We have to have some respect for ourselves."

"Just because it hasn't been done doesn't mean it can't be done."

There was something to ponder. Why couldn't we use multiple languages in headlines and copy? Our reader would understand it, so what was to hide?

"JACK DONE GOOD," said Kal. "Man, that is so boring."

Zak typed in the words and they filled the page perfectly. "Kal done good," said Akeel.

"And to balance it out a bit we will begin the story with….'The much-maligned Blackburn MP has been praised by all sections of the community'…"

"What do you mean much maligned? Who said he is maligned?" I said.

Zak chuckled to himself. "You did, remember. You didn't want us to lick anyone's arses."

Akeel and I both nodded in tandem and Imran laughed. Kal shook his head. "It just doesn't make any sense."

Every half hour we would walk outside to have a cigarette. It broke things up, but it wasn't without its pitfalls.

Zak wasn't impressed. "We don't have time for fag breaks, lads. This paper isn't going to print itself."

"You can't take away a man's fag breaks. It is what we are?"

"There will be plenty of time to smoke once this paper is printed," added Zak.

The cigarette break helped to clear the mind before the next task, but Zak was right: we were spending more time outside smoking than trying to complete the task in hand.

Rather than admit that I was wrong, I did always try to find another excuse for my predicament. "Whose fucking idea was it to pick a paper factory for an office? I mean, we can't even smoke inside."

I knew when Kal wasn't happy with what I said as he would just stay silent.

"Just have your cigarette and get your arse back in here. And shut the door. Bloody freezing in here."

"Do you know what we could with in here?" I said, and before anyone could answer I added, "A bed settee."

A bed setee was a common piece of furniture found in many Asian households and was a combination of a bed, a fold out bed and a storage space. "We sit on it, sleep on it and put our pads in it."

As the clock struck one, Steely Dan's Do It Again played on the radio and I turned it up loud. Akeel began to shake his head, mimicking a Qawwali band member.

"Okay, we have a problem here, lads," I said.

The printer had jammed. "Who is good with their hands?"

Akeel got up, still shaking his head, walked over to the printer and then walked off towards the toilets. Kal and Imran began to fix the printer. "Yeah, we will sort it."

"We need that printer working, lads or we are in trouble," said Zak.

Proofing pages at night is not as easy as it first looked. In the beginning everyone was eager to check their words in print. Twenty-eight days later the sight of a page was starting to cause us to panic.

Imran had now left us as he had a real job to go to in the morning.

"I am never doing this bollocks again," I said. "What time do we have to finish this?"

Zak was busy proofing yet another page. "We have to get out of here by 7am and straight to the printers."

"Never going to happen. This is like some sort of slow torture. This can't be the life of a newspaper person."

I liked to make up terms and phrases to describe people and roles.

Zak stretched and yawned. "There is no such thing as a newspaper person. Keep checking the pages."

Kal as always was more positive. "It will get done. Don't worry, bro."

As was Akeel. "Just get on with it. This is the big test."

"How we spelling this name?" Kal got up and placed an A4 sheet of paper on the desk in front of me. "Vau-ghan."

I glanced at the name he had written in pencil. "It is pronounced Vaughan (Waun), as in the guy from The Man from UNCLE, Robert Vaughan."

Zak nodded as Akeel picked up the sheet. "No, that is Vaughn. That is different."

"Didn't he come in the A-team?" asked Zak.

"No, that was Hannibal Smith," said Kal.

Akeel was quick to correct him again. "He did come in the A-team as Stockwell the general and Hannibal Smith was George Peppard."

Kal sat back down at his desk. "Come on, boys, we can't be spelling any names wrong. What it is it? Is it Vau-ghan or Vaughn?"

"There is no such name as Vau-ghan," added Zak. "It is like saying Akh-taar when it is Akh-tar or baath when it is bath."

"Or Akhtaraah." I laughed to myself.

Kal was getting a little frustrated. "I am not bothered how we pronounce it, all I want to know is how it is spelt. Is it Vau-ghan or Vaughn?"

"We could ring her?" I proposed.

"It is 2.15am," said Zak. "Hello I am calling from Asian Image and we just wanted to know how you spell your name? I think it is Vau-ghan but my colleague here thinks you may be related to that guy from The Man from UNCLE or General Stockwell in the A-Team – Robert Vaughn."

"Okay, I got an idea, have you got a phonebook?" Akeel walked over to the fridge and reached for the Yellow Pages and then a phonebook and began to skim through the names. "Yes, it is Vaughan. I can't see any other Vaughans in Blackburn. We will go with Vaughan."

"Are you sure, Akeel?" I wasn't convinced. "That was pretty quick skimming there."

Akeel laughed and quickly placed the book back on the fridge. "Look, just go with Vaughan. It sounds about right."

Music was our company for a while.

It was now close to 3am and Olivia Newton John's version of 'Take me Home, Country Roads' was playing on the radio.

I walked over and turned it up.

Imran was deep in thought and continued to read some sheets on his desk. He then inadvertently began to hum along and then sing along to the words. I glanced across at Zak, Kal and Akeel.

"Country Roads, Take me Home to the place I belong, West Virginia…"

He didn't notice us watching him. Maybe he was lost in a moment completely on his own and the words resonated to him more than anyone else in that room at that moment.

Imran stopped singing and looked around at us all. "I love that song."

Proofing pages is a pain when you haven't slept. On the front page I spotted a glaring error and it wasn't the first time this had happened tonight. "Who wrote this piece about taxis?"

"Why?" asked Zak.

"You accidentally used 'cock' on the front page." I got up and put the sheet of paper in front of him.

Zak stared at it. "Where? There's no cock here."

"Not a cock. The word cock." I pointed to the offending word. "Here."

Akeel laughed out loud and leaned over to check the sheet. "It is there. There is a cock on the front page. We have a cock on the front page of Asian Image."

"And long may that continue," added Kal.

Zak, who up until then had been pointing out our mistakes, seemed visibly embarrassed. "Oh shit. Yeah. It's you guys, you keep talking and it is putting me off."

I picked up the page and walked around the office raising my voice. "Safety truce means Asian cocks safe."

Akeel chuckled. "Jobs… jobs… change that to jobs."

"Okay, okay… just keep checking," said Zak.

Kal got up from his seat. "How do you get that mixed up. Jobs and cocks." And paused. "Oh yeah… I can see that now."

"Okay, I need something for page 2." Akeel placed a sheet on the desk in front of me.

I looked at it and handed it back to him. "I am too tired now."

Zak walked across the room to pick up the sheet. "Yeah, we need something for that gap."

Everyone looked around at one another and I decided I had had enough and closed my eyes.

"It's cold, isn't it?" said Kal. "Eid. It's going to be cold."

Zak sat back down at his desk. "What do you mean?"

"It is going to be the coldest Eid ever since records began."

"How would you know that?" said Akeel.

"Work it out, "said Zak. "When is the last time we had Eid in January? You would have to go back more than 30 years."

Akeel began to calculate the dates. Eid was celebrated ten days earlier each year and having done so said, "So, what was the weather back in 1963?"

"I don't know," said Kal. "But neither does anyone else."

Zak laughed. "So, this will be the coldest Eid we ever experienced. Which fucker is going to tell us otherwise."

My eyes remained closed. "Listen boys, that is the biggest load of bullshit I have heard, but I have to say that also makes perfect sense. I will write it, Zak."

I got up, stretched and began to write. "British Muslims will suffer the coldest Eid since the early sixties if weather reports are to be believed.

"Temperatures will fall below zero Celsius on the night of Wednesday January 28 and the morning of January 29 says the regional Met Office in Manchester."

Akeel peered over my shoulder. "Don't forget about how cold it will be for people wearing shalwar kameez when they go to mosque in the morning."

I glanced up at him. "You really think about the common man, don't you? Yeah okay."

Several minutes later the final story was finished.

"There you go, Zak, finish that off."

Zak sat down in front of the computer and typed, COLDEST EID IN BRITAIN EVER.

We stood around the computer screen and stared at the finished page.

"Excellent," said Zak. "Coldest Eid ever since records began."

It was more morning than night as Akeel and Zak hurried over to the fridge to pour themselves some water.

"I got some samosas for Sehri, lads," said Zak. Each and every night whenever we had decided to stay behind long into the night, Zak and Akeel had taken it in turns to bring some food in to 'close' the fast. It had to be the most endearing and memorable moments of the whole past few weeks. Today, the meat samosas tasted a lot better for some reason.

Much like the previous days, we had to get out of the toilet paper factory before the first shift workers made an appearance at 7am. It was now 6am and we packed up the sheets of paper.

As dawn broke, the newspaper was complete. There was a part of us trying to be proud of what we had achieved, but tiredness kind of took over all other emotions at this time.

In the freezing morning chill, Wildchild, Renegade Master played loudly in the car. I looked over to Zak and turned the track off and we sat silently making our way across the Pennines to the Huddersfield Examiner to print the first edition of the Asian Image. Despite the lack of sleep, we seemed pretty upbeat as we were invited into the production room, which I had immediately nicknamed the dungeon.

I was again expecting the familiar conversation where we would have to explain we were not just a bunch of amateurs but the production staff at the Examiner were quite the opposite. They almost seemed thankful they had some new company, and the conversation was jovial as they scanned through our first meagre efforts into the world of publishing. "This is good stuff," said one of the staff as he spotted 'The Last Bit'.

There seemed to be some sort of unspoken 'code of the publishers'. You knew the other guy was tired and had had a long night so best to keep the conversation light and the questions to a minimum.

Printing the newspaper was an anti-climax if I was going to be completely honest. There was no real joy at seeing the first copy coming off the presses. There were no celebrations. It was done and it was time to move on.

38 ONE NIGHT IN BLACKBURN

Five thousand newspapers is a lot of newspapers.

Sleep is something you miss only when you don't get enough of it. Just over a month after having been sat in a takeaway, we headed out onto the streets of Blackburn to distribute our first edition.

We gathered on Victoria Street to map out how we were going to 'get rid' of all of the newspapers in the next 12 hours.

Kal opened up the boot of the car and then the back doors to reveal packs of newspapers. They were piled into every crevice of the car and hot paper smell wafted out of the vehicle as we stood there motionless. I lit up a cigarette and Kal took it from my hand before I had a chance to put it into my mouth. "Shit," he sighed. "Five thousand is a hell of a lot of newspapers. How we going to do this?"

Akeel and Imran pulled up and stood next to us as we contemplated the task ahead of us. Akeel had a map of the town and had managed to split the whole job into zones. "Here are the streets and we pick our streets and get distributing," he explained, shining a small torch on the sheet which was spread across the hood of the red Mazda. "If we start now we should be finished by midnight."

"There is no way you will finish this by midnight," said Imran.

I leant over to study the map, illuminating a section with my cigarette lighter. "What about the posh areas of town?"

Akeel laughed. "There are no posh areas of town."

I breathed in and sighed again. It was not as cold as the recent nights, but there was still a chill in the air as I began to lift a bundle of papers out of the car and tried cutting the plastic ties with a key. Imran leaned over and clipped open the plastic ties. "It's easy when you know how."

I placed a handful of papers into carrier bags. "We couldn't get any proper bags so, everyone, put them in these Tesco bags."

Akeel picked up his share from the back seat and put them over his arm. "I don't do bags."

"And another thing." It was time to share some of my own advice. "You have to be like Santa Claus."

"You mean Baba Christmas," said Imran.

"Yeah that guy too." I looked over at each of the others one at a time. "What I was about to say was we need to be like Santa Claus, nice, quiet and work stealth mode."

Akeel turned to me. "Oh bhai look around you, nobody here believes in Father Christmas."

Kal shook his head. "Come on, everybody believes in Father Christmas."

Imran laughed. "I feel sorry for the poor kid who wrote a letter to the North Pole wishing for a newspaper this year only for it to be delivered a month late."

We set off and headed towards Altom Street. "Did you lock your car, Kal?" I asked.

"Lock my car?" said Kal. "In case someone steals our precious papers?"

We raced through the first few houses and then turned on to Inkerman Street. "I hate this fucking hilly town," I exclaimed. "Why did we have to live in a hilly town? When our parents came over, did they not think this was a shithole of a place to live? Couldn't they have headed to LA and then maybe settle there?"

Akeel laughed. "How are you going to distribute these in South Central LA? They shoot your Paki arse at the first house."

"Anybody seen Zak? I knew it when it came down to it, he would make a run for it," I said handing a paper to a passer-by. "He had better do Midsummer Street."

Kal paused and looked at the sheet of streets written on a piece of paper. "Okay, let's get on with it. It has to be done one way or another. I will go with Akeel and you wait for Zak."

"Why do you get Akeel?"

"Akeel is a machine. Twat will do a whole street in double quick time."

Akeel was indeed a 'machine' and never ever got tired during our hikes.

I stopped. "Okay, we swap partners."

Kal laughed. "Just like old times."

Akeel grimaced, "Oh maan. I don't even want to know."

At that moment Zak pulled up and got out of his car, wrapped up and wearing a balaclava.

"Check this pudu out," laughed Akeel.

"What the hell, Zak?" I said.

"Why, Zak?" added Imran.

Zak rubbed his hands together. "It's just a bit chilly and I think I am coming down with something."

Akeel was not convinced. "Just take off the balaclava. Who cares? We are just delivering the papers."

"Like I said it is a bit cold," insisted Zak and he took several pre-bagged newspapers from his own car.

Delivering newspapers was not what we expected to be doing at this stage in our lives but here we were on a cold winter evening doing just that. I mean, it is one thing trying to build a reputation up for yourself and then being seen on the streets posting papers.

"Leave him alone," I said. "He's doing a male veil thing to protect himself from prying eyes."

"From you fucking pervs," said Kal.

"I can't be classed as a pervert. I may be physically a dirty man as I bathe only on Sundays but a pervert I am not."

"You only bathe once a week?" asked Zak

"Nobody else only bathe on Sundays?" I looked at the others as we made our way up a street. "The jug and bucket? I thought Sunday was bathing day?"

We did not have a shower at home and still used a jug and bucket to have a wash. This may seem a little strange to some people, but I had presumed everyone else bathed the same way until I used a shower for the first time at the swimming centre. No one batted an eyelid at the 'jug and bucket' suggestion but were more interested in the number of times I bathed.

"I do Sundays and Wednesdays," said Kal.

"Aren't you special!" joked Imran.

We all looked at Akeel. "If you must know, then once a month."

I laughed and Zak made a muffled sound from underneath his balaclava before lowering it to speak: "Dirty bastards."

Zak and I made our way through a series of terraced streets and once we had finished one stretch we nipped through the dark alleyways to the next street.

"This is an amazing street, isn't it," I said, gazing up Shear Brow. "Nothing like it anywhere on the planet. I know I take the piss sometimes but this is one hell of a town. Look how beautiful it is… It is like some majestic mountain we must journey up and traverse to reach the promised land."

Zak stood next to me and stared up towards one of the steepest hills in town. The streets were still busy with people hurrying from home to home as the month of Ramadan was coming to an end.

Zak folded several newspapers. "To reach the promised land you have to make it up the gardens too."

I sighed. "Yeah. Fucker. What a shit street."

Shear Brow was not a typical street. Whilst many rows and rows of terraced homes are built on steep inclines, this stretch of homes had front gardens to test even the most determined 'delivery boy'.

"This *will* work, won't it, Zak?"

"It will, don't worry." He didn't sound as confident as a week ago though.

"What kind of journalist writes the paper, prints the paper and then delivers the paper? We have to do this every month?"

I couldn't imagine anyone else doing this.

"Until we get some delivery people, yes."

"I would rather deliver it myself – at least I know it is done." I knew how this game worked. It was all very well saying you were delivering the papers but a different thing trusting someone else who may dump them in a back alley.

Reaching the top of the road I nipped into a side street. I was about to post a paper when the door opened and a young woman stood there. "News-paper," I said slowly.

"Thank you," she replied.

"Asian paper, you know. Free. Tell Dad."

She looked at me with a level of disdain. "I may dress like a freshie, but I can speak English just fine."

I felt embarrassed but I had my follow up line ready, "So then…," but before I could finish the sentence she slammed the door in my face.

I met Zak moments later. "What?" He looked at me with a puzzled look on his face.

"This isn't bad at all really once you get the hang of it. From now on I am only doing the houses on this side of the street – it is where the good looking people live."

Zak handed me some more papers. "I dread to think where the ugly people are."

Several streets later I joined Kal along another steep incline, and we came across two elderly men in long black coats leaving a house.

"Asalamulaikum Khalil teek eh?" said the first man whom we recognised as Sajad Saab.

"Yes, uncle. Here, take a newspaper." Kal folded and then handed over a copy.

"What is this?" said the second old man. "You have started a new newspaper delivery service?"

Kal was quick to point out that we were in fact a lot more accomplished than that. "No, it is a newspaper, we are publishing the whole thing."

As a front room light was switched on and the light shone on to our faces, he recognised us. "I thought you two went to university? What is this job you are doing?"

His friend had more of a sarcastic attitude. "You spent all that time in university and here you are delivering newspapers at night. What did you get a degree in? Newspaper delivery? What a waste of education this was."

Both of the men laughed. It was also customary to share one's own success in life and find a way to demean someone else. Sajad Saab chuckled again. "This is the same dogs' work we did when we came here. My lad never went to university and now runs two stores. Has a house and a car too. Maybe you could learn a thing or two from him."

"Graduate paper boys!" added his friend, who I was actually was warming to. I mean he was a son of a bitch but boy did he know how to demoralise people he had just met.

Sajad Saab decided it wasn't enough to talk us down and decided to say it Punjabi: "Mera Puttar degree lay kar delivery karda hai. (My son got himself a degree and delivers papers)."

Both men chuckled again to themselves and began to walk off down the hill.

I stood there silently not entirely sure what to say. They had a point – we had gone through the education system but we had ended up doing the same jobs as our parents.

I glanced across at Kal who had that disappointed look on his face. It was a look I had seen many a time over the years and I knew right then he was about to say something quite wonderful. "Well, have a read anyway and maybe give a copy to your fraudy son," he said as both men turned around, "who we both know is banging that fat bird who is also his auntie." And then he muttered out of sheer frustration, "Stupid lans (dicks)."

Both men thankfully didn't quite hear him swear but in all honestly I wish they had done. "Chal (let's go)."

With Eid on the horizon, a number of shops were open. "Wait one minute, Kal, wait here."

I walked into a store to see 'Book girl' who was familiarly sat behind the counter reading. "You did it then."

I wiped my nose with the top of my hand and then showed off my hands which were tainted with black ink. "Yes, there you go," handing her a copy.

She placed her book down and leant over the counter to pick out another copy from the bag. "Maybe I will take a fresh one."

"Okay then," she said.

"Okay, I will see you."

"Yes indeed."

I left the shop and Kal was smoking yet another cigarette. "Who was that?"

"That, my good friend, is our salvation."

We stopped at a few more shops and stores along the route, dropping off twenty to thirty copies at each address. It felt encouraging seeing customers pick up a newspaper as we left it on the counter, and several times I would stand near the doorway and peer back into the shop to find out who read it first. It also turns out this was a far more efficient way to distribute papers and far less taxing.

I popped into a barber's which was still open ahead of the Eid rush and then posted four copies into a launderette. People will read anything if they are bored out of their skulls.

A short walk to the bottom of a busy street and we both stopped in our tracks as we spotted 'Rasputin' heading towards us. He was wearing his trademark shalwar kameez and long jacket with a black wholly hat.

"Hey, look," I whispered and lit up another cigarette.

Rasputin stopped and stared at us both. "Assalamualaikum, brothers."

"Waalaikumussalam, brother," replied Kal almost sarcastically.

I folded a newspaper and handed it to him. "You might like this."

Rasputin took the paper from me and smiled. "Thanks. Looks good." He wiped his nose with the top of his knuckles, turned and headed off up the road.

It was like meeting your idol and then clamming up. "Why didn't you ask him his real name," I said.

"Why didn't you?"

"I can't believe it," I said excitedly. "Wait till I tell the rest we gave an Asian Image to Rasputin."

It had already been a very tiring night, but meeting Rasputin had been a real highlight and gave us that extra burst of energy we needed.

We headed along London Road and met up with Zak again. Walking towards us in the opposite direction was Councillor Faisel.

"Oh shit," I said. "Just what we need."

"Asalamuliakum, my dear friends. The newspaper is out. Wonderful. Let me help you."

Kal and Zak shook hands with Councillor Faisel who proceeded to take some copies from our bags. "Let me help you distribute these."

Kal looked at me. "Oh that's really kind of you, uncle."

The funny thing is he did not open the paper to see if his picture had been printed.

"Give to me. I will do this street for you and if you have any left give to me and you can leave in my shops."

He walked with a spring in his step and stopped a vehicle to hand them a copy.

"Okay then," I said clearly a little embarrassed. "That was actually very nice of him."

"Yeah." Zak paused, staring with some newfound trust in humanity. "It was, wasn't it."

Kal smiled at us both and shook his head.

Akeel was posting papers on an adjoining street and we spotted him sprint out of a garden as a dog barked behind him. "Penchod Khuta (dog) nearly got me."

"Was it an Al-station?" asked Kal. "They're the worst."

"It's pronounced Al-sation, you stupid idiot," pointed out Akeel and then he lifted his left foot to reveal some dog faeces. He muttered to himself and proceeded to scrape off the muck on the side on a pavement. He then took a newspaper out from his small pile and wiped the remainder of the muck from the sole of his shoe and scrunched up the paper. He looked up at us both staring at him in horror. "Oh yeah, sorry, lads."

Kal paused wiped his nose with his sleeve for what seemed like the twentieth time tonight. "Just don't deliver that one."

The evening wore on and every so often someone would stop us and talk about the content the next issue should include. "Hey," I heard a voice behind us as we walked past a store. I turned to see a young woman with a headscarf holding a copy of the newspaper. "Are you guys distributing this?"

Kal was about to speak but I thought it best if I took the glory for a change. "Yeah that's us. How can we help?"

"Well," she said, "don't take offence to this, but you can start by getting a proof-reader. My daughter can write better than this. You got loads of spelling mistakes in here. If a white person reads this, they are going to think our English is rubbish." She began to open up the newspaper. "And here on page two, how do you know it is going to be the coldest Eid ever? Are you a weatherman?"

I turned my head and pretended to look for something in my pocket, hoping she would see that I was busy and leave us alone.

Kal laughed. "Well then, newspaper boy, answer the nice lady."

"Yes well," I said. "It's been a tough night. We will try to fix these problems next month."

There was nothing worse than going through a whole night and being told your paper had mistakes in it. Despite that wonderful moment when we met Rasputin, things really couldn't be more depressing. "I like the article from the lawyer though," she said. I think she felt a little bad having pointed out our work was at best amateurish.

The evening was getting colder and it was also getting more and more difficult to grip a newspaper in your hands. We hurried from door to door and I watched Imran clamber over to post paper after paper and stand and chat to almost every person walking past.

I had just posted a paper and was heading towards the gate in a small estate and as I turned back I saw someone turn on the hallway light and then the door opened. "Oi, I don't want your Paki paper here." The man threw the paper to the ground in disgust.

I went back and picked up the newspaper and he shut the door in my face.

I reached the end of the garden and to see Akeel. "What happened?"

"Let's move on. He doesn't want our Paki paper."

Akeel had a blank look on his face and ran back into the garden posting not one but two copies back through the letterbox and then rushed back past me. "Fuck him."

This was not the first time someone had abused us tonight. Earlier a woman had got into an argument with Imran about the paper being racist and if she was 'permitted' to read it. Imran, who loved discussions of this nature, had spoken to her for several minutes, explaining to her to simply read it and if she didn't like any of the content to get in touch and we would endeavour to improve things in the next issue. It hadn't made much difference. "But your paper IS racist," she pointed out again.

Imran had given up on trying to explain himself to the woman, replying, "Maybe it is not the paper that is racist."

I caught up with him and handed him a lit cigarette. "Did you think it would be like this?"

"What?"

"This. Us. Here in the middle of the night distributing papers that no one is going to read."

Imran looked almost offended at my comment. Despite holding down a full-time job he had still made time for the venture out when it mattered. He was still there when it counted. "Of course they will read it. Some people are never going to like what you do or what you write because they don't like to be told what they believe.

"The only thing that matters is you don't forget this moment. This. Now. Walking down the street in the cold carrying newspapers in a Tesco bag. Walking through these alleyways. This is what matters."

Imran had a way of putting things into perspective.

"Can I ask you something?"

"Yeah, go on."

"That joke about the four people sleeping and their blind mate, where did you hear it?"

Imran chuckled to himself. "There was a guy in our village who would share these jokes with us. I suppose I robbed it from him. And he must have robbed it from someone else."

I stopped walking. "It's a fucking funny joke. You have to tell it to Kal and the boys later."

I joined Akeel in Audley Range – he had stopped outside a house and was watching TV through a window. "What's on?" I asked.

"I don't know. Something about animals."

The couple in the house suddenly stared up at us from their sofa, at which point Akeel waved and moved on. A passer-by stopped me to ask for a newspaper, walked a few yards and threw the paper on the ground after having flicked through it. I hurried behind and wanted to shout something really clever but just picked up the scattered sheets and stuffed them back in my bag.

"That's got to be the most depressing thing ever," said Akeel as he caught up with me. "You work your arse off and some son of a bitch does that. You couldn't make this shit up." He laughed out loud again. "Let's go."

A car pulled up in front of us as the lights turned red. Tupac and Dr Dre's 'California Love' played loudly as a man in a smart suit and bright tie nodded his head and blew cigarette smoke out through a small gap in the window. Akeel wiped his brow leaving a black ink mark on his forehead. "I used to like that tune when it meant something."

Every so often Akeel would just say some amazing things.

Akeel had teamed up with Zak again and were making good time in the terraced streets again as Kal and I headed to one of the darker areas of town. "Listen, Shuiab, we will go to Dundee Drive and you guys go to Shakeshaft Street," said Akeel.

Kal was getting visibly tired by this stage. "Where the fuck is Shakeshaft Street? There is a Shakeshaft Street in this town? Who names a street Shakeshaft?"

We parked up and, Tesco bags in hand, began to distribute some copies as a flash white Mercedes pulled up alongside us. It stopped and the driver side window opened and a waft of weed filled the cold night air.

"Oi, paperboys, give us a paper," said the driver as he turned his music down.

I coughed. "Yeah, sure here you go."

He opened up the newspaper and flicked through the pages before handing it on to his passenger. "You delivering this yourselves? Who is running this? Who is the main man in charge?"

I was about to say something before Kal intervened again. "We are just the delivery boys."

Both driver and passenger laughed as the back window wound down to reveal another back seat passenger behind the tinted glass. "A dangerous business to be in is this newspapers," said the driver. "Never know who you might piss off."

Kal stared at the driver. "Not the only dangerous business to be in, is it?"

"What's that supposed to mean?" The man smirked and glanced across at his passenger and stared back at Kal. I got the feeling he was hoping Kal would flinch, which he didn't. I mean, say what you want but you can't look tough stood in the middle of the street with a carrier bag full of free newspapers – but somehow he did.

A Nissan Bluebird pulled up alongside us and the window wound down to reveal Benny smoking a cigarette. "Alright, fuck faces, them papers been delivered yet?"

The driver looked across at Benny. "These mates of yours, Benny?"

Benny stroked his moustache. "Well, I wouldn't call them mates, but I know them."

I looked across at Benny and then back at the driver. Kal, meanwhile, hadn't taken his eyes off the driver.

Benny flicked his cigarette on the hood of the other vehicle. "Are you guys sticking around or do I need to get out of the car to piss in your petrol tank?"

The driver smirked again but this time a little more nervously, then turned the volume back up before slowly pulling away.

It seems some of what this small man said wasn't bravado after all. "Told you this was my town."

Benny took out another cigarette, lit it and drove off.

We crossed the road and continued to post papers into the homes and chose to ignore the fact that Benny had just intervened before things could have got ugly.

"Look at that," I said. "How the fuck is he driving a Merc and here I am delivering a newspaper at 2am."

It was a genuine observation if I was going to be honest. Here we were in the middle of the night in the freezing cold, wearing the same underpants we had had on for a week and there he was smoking weed in his nice warm car with his mates.

"He is what you would call a chicken neck, brother," replied Kal as we walked door to door. "You know, he has a neck like a chicken and thinks he is in a gangster movie and then goes home to have rotee salan (chapati and curry) at his mum's. The real gangsters don't drive in shitty Mercs, have tennis ball haircuts and wear gold chains."

"Yeah." I had dropped a copy near a gutter and bent down to pick it up. "Real gangsters deliver newspapers in the middle of the night."

The night was dragging now and there comes a time when the dream of doing something for yourself is replaced by a desire simply to get things done. Imran had already left us for the night as he had another early shift the next day. We, on the other hand, had to get these papers delivered and get home.

Delivering anything to homes at night comes with an added problem in that you have to be a little quieter when you approach homes. There can be nothing worse, I thought, than someone slamming your letterbox shut at some ungodly hour.

We met up with Akeel again and found ourselves on one of the town's busiest roads which was quiet.

I laughed. "Okay, Aki you going to get Bromley Street done for us."

Akeel was weary-eyed and looked like someone who had completed two marathons back-to-back. Akeel puffed out his cheeks and shook his head. "Whose bright idea was it to leave that to the end."

"Yours," said Kal.

The soles of my feet were aching as a police car pulled up alongside us. It was not the first time we had seen a police vehicle go past that night and personally I was happy enough seeing them doing their rounds.

"Good morning, gentleman," said the officer. "Now, where are you lot off to in the middle of the night?"

Even though I hadn't done anything I still felt we had, and wanted this vehicle to move on as quickly as possible.

"Just on a pleasant walk," said a nonchalant Kal.

"At 3am?" asked the officer.

Kal looked up at the night sky and then back at the officer. "Yeah. We thought it was a lovely night for a stroll."

The officer paused and stared at Kal and then at Akeel. "Okay, don't get wise with me, son. What's in the bags?"

"Papers," replied Akeel.

"What kind of papers?"

I knew Kal would find it difficult to resist humouring the question. "Rizla. There look. Happy now. Now leave us alone."

The police officer glanced across at his own partner and then back at us. "Newspaper. You are delivering newspapers? Why would you do that at this time."

I would have probably asked the same question if I am going to be honest, but three guys carrying carrier bags in the middle of the night was bound to attract some sort of attention. Maybe it was the tiredness. Maybe it was the fact that it was cold and the night had dragged on about six hours too long, but Akeel had finally had enough. He wiped his nose again with his sleeve. "Because we are three sad individuals whose lives have taken a turn for the worse and decided to write and then print a newspaper to give our pointless lives some sort of meaning." There was a blank look on his face. "Having spent three full days proof-reading pages and having imaginary conversations with a made up woman, we now find ourselves wandering the streets of this cold and desolate town at 3 o'clock in the morning delivering the bastard newspaper we have no idea if anyone will ever read. So, if you want to arrest three grown paperboys, please do so. At least I will get a lift back home."

Kal laughed whilst the officer nodded and paused.

"Okay then, we shall leave you to it then," the officer said and moved off.

I put my arm around Akeel. "Fucking poet you are."

Life is not always about returning to the place where you belong, it is about how you got there. As Akeel called it a night, Kal and I had found ourselves back on the streets where we had grown up and somehow it didn't feel the same.

"Okay then, back on Spring View, who would have thought it," he said, standing at the bottom of the road looking up towards the row of houses. "Let's get this finished."

He instantly recognised the house he had grown up in and paused for a while at the gate before taking the two steps into the front garden and leaning forwards and posting a newspaper. He then turned and looked at me further down the street.

We spent the next 30 minutes distributing the remaining papers from our bundles as we spotted a milkman on his morning routes. I was back on my childhood paper round as the cold and lack of sleep finally caught up with me. The same streets and the same houses, but a different me.

Over the past 12 years, the houses and cobbled streets had changed little; in fact, I would think they had gotten meaner and the steep hills even more exhausting. As a child it matters little whether you can complete the task, but you do it because you don't want to let anyone down. As you get older you like to think you do things for a different reason. I think I had purposely left the street I had grown up on until the end. It was a small terraced road that was blocked at the far side and the only way cars could get out was to go through a cobbled back alley.

Next door but one lived an elderly woman named Bertha who would visit our homes daily and acted more like a babysitter than a neighbour. Offer her some tea and light her cigarettes, and she could sit all day watching the TV or simply telling us about how the street used to be. I think she liked the company and my mother was more than obliging, despite her odd 'controversial' comment on migrants. People, it seemed, were more forgiving – or maybe they just didn't realise what those comments meant.

I paused outside my childhood home and waited to post the newspaper.

Kal was watching from the top of the street and shouted at me, "Oi, Come on."

The Very Last Bit

Akeel and Imran left soon after to pursue full-time roles, as did Zak, who also moved on two years later. The title was acquired by Newsquest in 2002.

Kal and Shuiab continued working together until 2003 when Kal took on a new challenge as head of an enterprise organisation. Shuiab remains a journalist at the Lancashire Telegraph and Asian Image.

Asian Image continued to be published every single month for 23 years, edited by Shuiab Khan. Dear Noreen was later renamed Dear Massi but The Last Bit remained The Last Bit. The title spawned several award ceremonies and sports tournaments helping to celebrate the contributions of the Asian community in the North West.

Jay, who was already a wonderful human being, went on to become an even better one.

About the author

Shuiab Khan, 47 is a journalist and columnist at the Lancashire Telegraph. He was born and schooled in Blackburn before studying Politics and Economics at the University of Loughborough, graduating in 1994. He went on to spend time in Manchester and then Ecuador in 1997. He returned to the UK the same year and in January 1998 helped to publish the free Asian Image newspaper in Blackburn. The edition was later distributed in other towns in the North West, including Manchester, Preston, Bolton and Burnley. In 2002 the title was acquired by Newsquest and Shuiab was employed to work as Editor of the Asian Image and a writer for the Lancashire Telegraph. A keen footballer and Blackburn Rovers supporter, he has also helped to organise a range of North West amateur sporting events since 1998.

In 2013 Shuiab launched the Asian Media Awards aiming to highlight the contribution of journalists, broadcasters, presenters, actors and media professionals from across the UK.

www.ingramcontent.com/pod-product-compliance
Lightning Source LLC
LaVergne TN
LVHW051110080426
835510LV00018B/1982